£7.50

Beginner's Guide
To Seaweeds

Also by C. L. Duddington

BEGINNER'S GUIDE TO BOTANY

Beginner's Guide
To Seaweeds

C. L. Duddington

PELHAM BOOKS

First published in Great Britain by
PELHAM BOOKS LTD
52 Bedford Square
London, W.C.1
1971

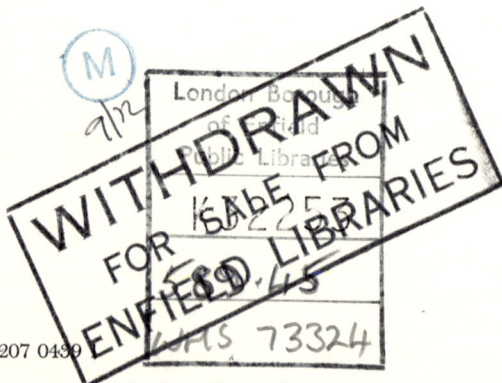

Set and printed in Great Britain by
Ebenezer Baylis & Son Ltd, The Trinity Press,
Worcester, and London, in Bell eleven on twelve point,
on paper supplied by P. F. Bingham Ltd
and bound by James Burn at Esher, Surrey

Contents

Preface

In this book I have attempted to provide an introduction to the very heterogeneous group of plants known as seaweeds. The seaweeds seem to be rather neglected by the amateur botanist; people who can give a name to almost any wild flowering plant are often completely stumped when asked to identify even as common a seaweed as the toothed wrack. I think this is partly because all seaweeds appear, at a casual glance, to be the same; the fact that they are not becomes obvious only on close inspection. The lives of seaweeds are mysterious to most people; they have no seeds, and to observe their reproduction closely we need a microscope. That is why they are included in the great group of plants that are still called cryptogams (*crypto*, hidden; *gam*, marriage), along with the fungi, the liverworts and mosses, and the ferns and their allies.

My aim in writing this book is to persuade a few people to look a little more closely at seaweeds the next time they take a holiday near the seaside. If they do, I am sure they will be pleasantly surprised. As the book is addressed to non-botanists, I have tried to use everyday language as far as possible. There are many things in connexion with seaweeds, however, that cannot be expressed without the use of scientific jargon. I have kept the use of this to a minimum, and all scientific terms are explained in the Glossary at the end of the book.

Most people these days have at least an elementary smattering of biology. For those who have no knowledge at all it might perhaps be best if they were to read the Appendix first; this gives an outline of the concepts of cell and nucleus without which any book on a biological subject would hardly be intelligible.

If, as a result of reading this book, a few readers begin to take an interest in seaweeds, I shall be more than repaid for the time it took in the writing.

Kingston-upon-Thames   C.L.D.

List of Illustrations

9

```
**** 
* 1 *
****
```

Introduction to the seaweeds

We are all familiar with seaweeds; the word conjures up memories of summer days by the seaside, with the bladder wrack, one of the commonest of the brown seaweeds, crackling as we walk over it. Many of us have, at one time or another, brought home a specimen of the sea belt, or poor man's weather glass (*Laminaria saccharina*), to use as a rough barometer. If the frond felt moist and limp it was going to rain, whereas if it remained brittle to the touch we felt we could rely on the weather keeping fine.

These are but two of the 800-odd seaweeds, or marine algae, that have been recorded as occurring around the shores of Britain. Some, like the bladder wrack, are very common indeed; others occur but rarely, perhaps at one particular point only on our coastline. Some are large; the bladder wrack is one of the bigger British seaweeds, though it is but a dwarf beside some of the gigantic Pacific kelps. Others are so small that a fairly powerful microscope is needed to make them visible at all. Some, like the bladder wrack, are brown in colour, while others may be green, yellow, orange, red, or even blue.

What are seaweeds? Botanically, they are plants belonging to the group known as algae—the group that also includes what an Irishman is reported to have called "fresh-water sea-weeds". As members of the algae they have certain things in common. They are plants which are not divisible into stem, root, and leaf; their bodies consist of what is called a thallus. They do not reproduce by means of seeds, but instead have simpler reproductive bodies called spores. They all live in the sea or in brackish water. This last point may seem too obvious to deserve mention, but in fact a few seaweeds, such as the channelled wrack (*Pelvetia caniculata*), live so far up the beach

15

that they may be reached only by the highest spring tides.

One other important feature that the seaweeds have in common is that, with the exception of a very few microscopic forms, they all contain the green pigment chlorophyll—the pigment that makes plants green. True, the green colour may not be apparent, for most of the seaweeds also possess other pigments whose colour masks the green of the chlorophyll. That the chlorophyll is there can easily be seen if a portion of the frond of the sea belt is left in a bucket of water for a few hours, for the brown pigment diffuses out in patches, leaving the seaweed a piebald green.

The possession of chlorophyll means that, like other green plants, the seaweeds are independent of organic food, since they are able to manufacture their own organic compounds from carbon dioxide dissolved in the sea water, with the aid of sunlight as a source of energy, the chlorophyll trapping the energy in sunlight and making it do chemical work. The process is called photosynthesis, and from the sugar produced in this way the seaweed is able to synthesize all the other complex organic compounds that it needs.

Photosynthesis needs light, and as we go deeper in the water the intensity of the light is rapidly diminished. Even in the clear water of the Mediterranean, no seaweed can grow at a depth greater than about 600 feet.

The range of size shown by the seaweeds is greater than that of any other group of organisms. On the one hand, the minute floating life of the sea, known as the plankton, contains tiny seaweeds consisting of single cells no more than 10μ in diameter. The symbol μ stands for the microscopist's unit of measurement, and is equal to one thousandth of a millimetre, or one twenty-five-thousandth of an inch. At the other extreme, the giant kelp *Macrocystis*, which lives in the Pacific Ocean, has a frond that may be 600 feet long. This is the greatest length—though not the greatest bulk—attained by any plant, for the Douglas fir, giant among trees, can only boast of a height of just over 400 feet.

One might expect to find gigantic seaweeds such as *Macrocystis* growing in tropical seas, but this is not the case; they prefer the cooler waters of the Pacific off the coast of California. Not that there is any lack of tropical species, for seaweeds are to be found in every sea, from the Equator to the Poles.

Few people realize how many seaweeds inhabit the oceans of the world, for the vast majority of them belong to the plankton: microscopic seaweeds that float in the sea in countless billions, far too small to be noticed except by the small crustaceans, molluscs, and other forms, of animal life that eat them. Statistics, however, reveal their vast numbers. Seventy-one per cent of the surface of the earth is covered by sea, and it has been calculated that the oceans of the world produce about 3·2 tons of dry plankton per acre every year. This compares favourably with crops grown upon land. A good corn crop averages no more than 2·6 tons fresh weight per acre. Sugar beet, the heaviest crop of all in terms of weight alone, produces no more than 13 tons per acre. Even if we allow that a land crop grows only on the surface of the ground while the sea has three dimensions, these figures are still impressive. Every time we accidentally take a mouthful of sea water while bathing we are swallowing a few million planktonic seaweeds.

The abundance of phytoplankton, as the planktonic seaweeds are called, is important, because the phytoplankton is the ultimate basis of all life in the sea. These tiny organisms are the food of small crustacea, such as copepods, which are the principal food of many kinds of fishes; without them the small animal life in the sea, and consequently the fishes, could not live. The phytoplankton, being photosynthetic, does not need organic food; it is the starting point of all the different food chains that end with fishes. More will be said about this aspect of marine economy in a later chapter.

The value of the marine phytoplankton in providing food for fishes far transcends all other uses to which seaweeds may be put, but some of the larger seaweeds are not without their value. Seaweeds as a food for man and beast have been known since before the dawn of history, and in modern times the Japanese run seaweed farms for the cultivation of edible seaweeds. Kelp burning used to be a thriving business, first as a source of soda, and later of potash and iodine; these uses have now been replaced by the production of alginic acid and the alginates, which is far more profitable. Seaweed is used in the production of agar-agar, used in media for cultivating fungi and bacteria in every biological laboratory in the world. Seaweed makes excellent manure for farm and garden, in which role it is not exploited to the extent that it should be in these days when dung is scarce. These are only a few examples of the uses of seaweeds which will be dealt with more fully later.

Botanists divide seaweeds into eight major groups or phyla, and the colour of the seaweed plays an important part in this classification. This may seem somewhat arbitrary, for colour is not usually regarded as being of particular importance in plant systematics, but the seaweeds differ from most other plants in that their pigmentation does seem to indicate something fundamental in their biochemical make-up.

The characteristic green colour of plants in general is due to the presence in plant cells of minute bodies called chloroplasts. These have a complex structure. Examination under the electron microscope, an instrument producing extremely high magnifications, has shown that a chloroplast consists of a colourless body, the stroma, in which chlorophyll-containing particles, known as grana, are embedded. The structure of the grana is also complex. A single granum is built up on the same plan as a multi-decker sandwich, with layers of protein and lipoid (fatty material). The combined effect of the grana makes the whole chloroplast appear green, just as the effect of the multitudes of chloroplasts contained in its cells makes the whole plant appear green,

The story is further complicated by the fact that there are two sorts of chlorophyll commonly found in plants: chlorophyll a, which is blue-green, and chlorophyll b, which has a yellow-green hue. The chloroplasts of all plants except seaweeds contain about three times as much chlorophyll a as chlorophyll b, the mixture producing a grass-green colour. In the seaweeds the pigmentation is more complex, as other forms of chlorophyll, known as chlorophyll c, chlorophyll d, etc., also occur.

In addition to chlorophyll, the chloroplasts of seaweeds and other plants alike contain other pigments. There are the xanthophylls, which are compounds of carbon, hydrogen, and oxygen, and there are also the carotenes, which contain carbon and hydrogen alone. The xanthophylls are orange-yellow in colour, while the carotenes are brick-red; the red colour of carrots, for instance, is due to the presence of carotenes.

The business of plant pigmentation is far from simple, and in the seaweeds it is even more complex. For one thing, the chloroplasts in the seaweeds are often much larger than those of other plants; in some instances, particularly among the green seaweeds, there may be only one chloroplast per cell. Also, in addition to the chlorophylls, xanthophylls, and carotenes there may be other pigments to add their colours to the rainbow. The brown seaweeds, for instance, contain an additional brown pigment called fucoxanthin, while the red seaweeds have two additional pigments, phycoerythrin (red) and phycocyanin (blue). According to the relative amounts of the different pigments contained in its chloroplasts, or chromatophores as they are often called, a seaweed can be any colour of the rainbow.

The eight phyla into which the seaweeds are commonly divided are given below:

CHLOROPHYTA

These are the grass-green seaweeds. They are the seaweeds which most resemble the other green plants, and there is little or no doubt that the rest of the green plants were evolved from them. The range of form is extremely varied: some consist of a single cell, others are filamentous, while a few have a flattened, leaf-like structure. Among the latter, the sea lettuce (*Ulva lactuca*) is a familiar sight on British shores. Many of the Chlorophyta live in fresh water, and a few genera, such as *Cladophora*, have both fresh- and salt-water species. This is unusual, for the members of a genus of algae are usually all confined to fresh or salt water, but not both.

The Chlorophyta often have large chromatophores of complex structure. When they store up reserve food for future use it is usually in the form of starch; this is another point of resemblance to the higher plants.

EUGLENOPHYTA

These are small organisms consisting of a single cell, which swim by means of a whip-like process, or flagellum, projecting from the front end of the organism. The Euglenophyta may be marine, or they may be found in brackish or fresh water, or in the soil. The marine Euglenophyta form part of the phytoplankton.

CHRYSOPHYTA
This is a phylum which consists of three classes: the Xanthophyceae or yellow-green algae, the Chrysophyceae or golden-brown algae, and the Bacillariophyceae or diatoms. They may be unicellular or filamentous, marine or fresh-water. The relationship between the three classes in the Chrysophyta is not at all obvious, and some authorities would elevate each of the classes into a phylum in its own right. The diatoms have long been familiar as subjects for microscopy on account of the delicate ornamentations on their shells, and they are of great importance as the most numerous members of the marine phytoplankton.

PYRROPHYTA
This group consists mainly of unicellular flagellates, though colonial and filamentous forms occur occasionally. The Pyrrophyta are mainly marine, and they include the important group of dinoflagellates (Dinophyceae), which make up a considerable part of the marine phytoplankton.

CRYPTOPHYTA
This small phylum of flagellate organisms, mainly unicellular but occasionally forming colonies, is scantily represented both in marine and fresh waters.

PHAEOPHYTA
These are brown seaweeds, a phylum which includes the common wracks and kelps, including the giant kelp *Macrocystis*. Most of the brown seaweeds are large, though there are also some microscopic forms. Nearly all the brown algae are marine. The chromatophores of the phaeophyta contain the yellow-brown pigment fucoxanthin.

RHODOPHYTA

These are the so-called red seaweeds, though they may in fact be of almost any colour. Their chromatophores contain the red pigment phycoerythrin and the blue pigment phycocyanin, and according to the relative proportions of these, together with the chlorophylls, xanthophylls, and carotenes, they may appear any colour from red, through orange, yellow, and green, to blue. The Rhodophyta are mostly marine, occurring in rock pools on the shore, and below the low-tide mark; on the whole they prefer deeper water than the brown seaweeds. The red seaweeds usually have a complex structure made up from intricately interwoven filaments, and the details of their life histories are more complicated than those of any other seaweeds.

CYANOPHYTA

These are the blue-green algae. They are simple organisms, differing in many ways from all other plants. They contain phycocyanin in addition to chlorophylls, xanthophylls, and carotenes but these pigments are not contained in chromatophores. Their cells are without organized nuclei (the nucleus of a cell is a part of the protoplasm, or living matter of the cell, set apart to exert a controlling influence on the cell's activities; it is also the site of the genes or carriers of hereditary information). The Cyanophyceae contains marine, fresh-water, and soil-inhabiting species, and is an extremely ancient group.

```
****
* 2 *
****
```

The wracks

The wracks belong to the family of brown seaweeds known as
the Fucaceae. This family contains a number of our best known
seaweeds, such as the bladder wrack mentioned in the previous
chapter. They consist of large seaweeds which grow mainly on
rocky shores in the north temperate regions of the world; they
occur particularly in Europe and North America. They are less
common on sandy beaches, for they usually grow attached to
rocks by an organ called the holdfast, with their fronds floating
upwards in the water towards the light. Since they mostly grow
in the inter-tidal zone, they are usually uncovered by the tide
for at least part of the time, the period during which they are
exposed depending upon how near the high-tide mark they
grow.

The various species of wracks differ in the amount of expo-
sure they can stand. Some, like the channelled wrack (*Pelvetia
canaliculata*), grow so high up on the shore that they are actually
beyond the reach of all but the higher spring tides; for most of
the time they merely get splashed with spray when the tide
comes in. Others, such as the serrated wrack (*Fucus serratus*)
grow only near to the low-tide mark, for their needs include
immersion for the greater part of their lives.

A wrack usually consists of three parts: the holdfast by means
of which it clings to a rock, the stalk or stipe, which is a
cylindrical portion of varying length, and the frond, blade, or
lamina, call it what you will, which is the flat, expanded portion
which makes up most of the seaweed. The fronds of the wracks
are all more or less ribbon-shaped, often branching repeatedly
in one plane. They are usually tough and leathery, and their
colour can be anything from pale brown to almost black.

The wracks are usually perennial plants, but they tend to be rather short-lived, for they are exposed to the full fury of winter storms. It has been estimated that more than fifty per cent of the plants perish before reaching an age of three years, mainly owing to the pounding they get from the waves.

Most seaweeds exhibit two forms of reproduction: asexual, depending on the formation of reproductive bodies called spores, and sexual, consisting of the fusion of a pair of sex cells or gametes. The wracks are peculiar in not forming any spores; their reproduction is entirely sexual. The sex organs are formed on somewhat swollen areas near the tips of the branches of the fronds; these areas are called receptacles. The receptacles bear minute cavities called conceptacles, and within these cavities the sex organs are housed. The male sex organ is called an antheridium, and it produces the male gametes or sperms. The female organ is called the oögonium, and it contains the female gametes or egg cells. The sexual act consists of the fusion of a sperm with an egg cell, an event which usually takes place in the sea, and from the fertilized egg cell, which is called a zygote, a new seaweed grows.

Besides their sexual reproduction most of the wracks can reproduce vegetatively, a portion of the plant which happens to get broken off growing into a new plant. The power of vegetative reproduction possessed by the wracks is considerable.

The value of the wracks as manure has long been known, and in some districts they are even cultivated for this purpose. The "cultivation" is primitive in the extreme, and is usually undertaken on sandy beaches, for on rocky shores the supply of wracks is virtually inexhaustible. Pieces of rock, or large stones, are placed at intervals along the beach, at about half-tide mark. They quickly become colonized by fertile eggs brought in by the tide, and soon become covered with a growth of wracks, generally the bladder wrack. The plants are usually left for a year, after which they can be cut, the remains of the plants being left to rejuvenate and provide another crop. Sometimes the stones are turned over and a fresh crop is started.

The wracks were formerly burned on a large scale for the sake of the soda and potash they contain, but this is no longer carried out as more convenient sources have been found. They are, however, extensively used as a source of alginic acid and the alginates.

THE BLADDER WRACK

The bladder wrack (*Fucus vesiculosus*) is the most familiar, as well as the commonest, of all the wracks (Plate 1). It gets its name from the presence of air bladders in the fronds; these make the fronds buoyant, so that when the seaweed is submerged they float up towards the surface, thus taking full advantage of the available light. The bladders, which are about the size of small hazel nuts, are usually placed in pairs, one on each side of the frond.

The bladder wrack is extremely variable in form, and varies in length between one and five feet (Fig. 1). At one end is the holdfast, which is more or less disk-shaped. The cells on the

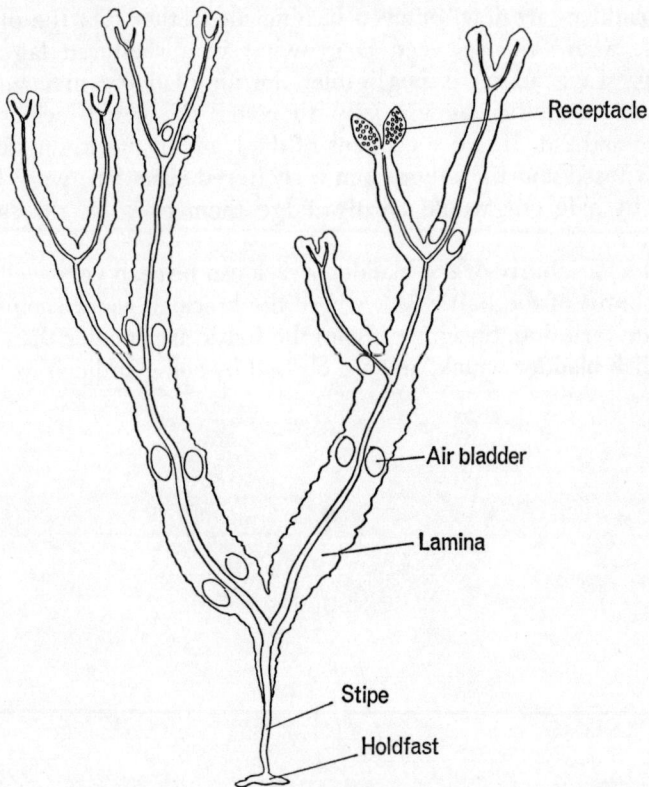

FIGURE 1.
The bladder wrack (Fucus vesiculosus).

lower side of the holdfast secrete a sticky mucus by which it becomes attached to a rock or stone, anchoring the plant securely and preventing it from being carried away by the action of the waves. Arising from the holdfast is the short stem or stipe, which is rounded and often branched at its upper end.

The greater part of the bulk of the bladder wrack consists of the frond, which is a flattened ribbon an inch or so in breadth, with a smooth margin. The frond forks repeatedly, a type of branching which is described as dichotomous. The frond bears the pairs of air bladders, which are variable in number. Where the bladder wrack is growing in an exposed situation, where it is much pounded by the surf, the branches of the frond are narrow, often no more than a quarter of an inch wide, and the air bladders are few, or even lacking altogether. On the other hand, where the seaweed is growing in a sheltered lagoon, where wave action is negligible, the air bladders may be so crowded together as virtually to cover the frond, which is broad and flat. If two specimens of the bladder wrack, one from an exposed and the other from a sheltered situation, were laid side by side one would hardly judge them to be of the same species.

The variability of the bladder wrack can be seen very well on the shores of the Baltic Sea, where the brackish water seems to favour variation. Specimens from the Baltic are smaller than the English bladder wrack, and are classed by some authorities as a

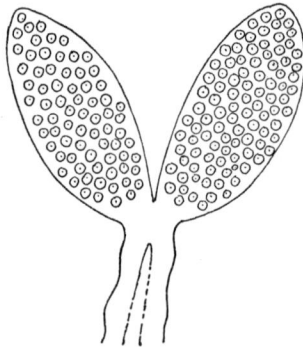

FIGURE 2

The tip of a fertile branch of the bladder wrack, showing a pair of receptacles.

separate variety, *Fucus vesiculosus* var. *balticus*. Other varieties of the bladder wrack have been described.

At the tips of the branches of the frond are the receptacles where the sex organs are housed (Fig. 2). These also are variable in form. They may be narrowly oval to almost rounded, and in some instances they are forked. When the sex organs are mature the receptacles are swollen, and mucilage oozes out of them. At maturity the tips of the fronds which bear the receptacles change in colour from the normal olive-brown to orange in the male plants, and yellowish-brown in the female plants.

If we cut a section (a thin slice) across the frond of the bladder wrack and examine it under the microscope, we can see that its structure is complex. The frond is covered by a single layer of cells called the meristoderm. These are rectangular in outline, and most of the chromatophores are concentrated in them. Beneath the meristoderm is the cortex, consisting of rounder cells with fewer chromatophores, and inside the cortex, occupying the centre of the frond, is the medulla. The medulla is built up of long filaments of cells placed end to end, and the filaments are embedded in mucilage. The filaments are not all the same. Some have thin walls, while in others the walls of the cells are thickened, and no doubt contribute to the strength of the frond.

The minute structure of the frond of the bladder wrack shows the principal of division of labour found in all but the smallest and most primitive plants. The meristoderm, for instance, is specialized for the work of photosynthesis. The thick-walled filaments in the medulla have a strengthening function, while the thin-walled filaments probably help in conducting food material elaborated in the meristoderm cells. The cortex is mainly padding, its presence increasing the area covered by the meristoderm, though the presence of chromatophores in its cells shows that it can also carry out a certain amount of photosynthesis.

If a section is cut across the stipe instead of the frond, much the same kind of structure is seen, the main differences being an enlargement of the medulla, with many more thick-walled filaments.

The reproductive organs of the bladder wrack are, as I have said, embedded in the receptacles. If we examine the surface of a

mature receptacle with the naked eye or, better, through a hand
lens, we can see a number of minute holes, through which
mucilage oozes when the sex organs are mature (Fig. 2).
These are the ostioles, or openings leading to the flask-shaped
chambers, or conceptacles, in which the reproductive organs are
placed. The bladder wrack is dioecious: that is, the male and
female sex organs are situated on different plants. In order to
see the details of the conceptacles it will be necessary to cut
a section through a receptacle for microscopic examination.

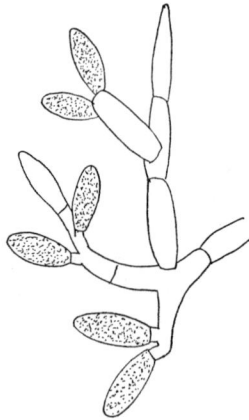

FIGURE 3.
*A branched hair from a male conceptacle of the bladder wrack, bearing
antheridia (stippled). Greatly magnified.*

The microscope shows us that the receptacle contains a
number of flask-shaped conceptacles, each connecting with the
exterior by an ostiole. The conceptacles are lined with hairs
called paraphyses; according to some authorities it is these hairs
that produce the mucilage that fills the conceptacles. If a receptacle was from a male plant, the male organs or antheridia will
be borne on the hairs; some will also be carried on the walls of
the conceptacle.

The antheridia are minute and club-shaped (Plate 2 and Fig.
3). Each at first contains a single nucleus, but this divides* into
two, the two into four, and so on until there are 64 nuclei

* See Appendix.

present. A certain amount of protoplasm collects round each nucleus, forming a male sex cell or gamete, provided with a pair of flagella by means of which it is able to swim.

The wall of the antheridium consists of two layers. When the gametes are ready to be liberated the outer wall splits open and the mass of gametes, still enclosed in the inner layer of the antheridium wall, squeezes out of the antheridium and passes into the mucilage which fills the conceptacle. Eventually it passes out, through the ostiole, into the sea water.

In a female conceptacle (Plate 3) the oögonia are carried on the conceptacle wall. Each oögonium consists of two cells: the oögonium proper and the stalk cell (Fig. 4). The single nucleus

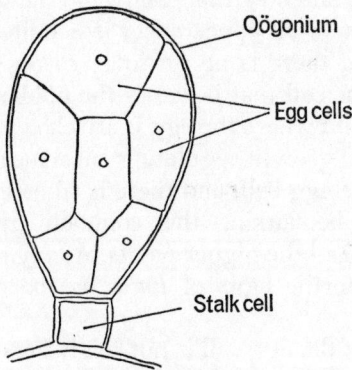

FIGURE 4.
An oögonium of the bladder wrack, greatly magnified.

of the oögonium divides three times, forming eight nuclei. Protoplasm collects round each nucleus, so that eight egg cells are formed.

The wall of the oögonium has three layers. When the eggs are ripe the two inner walls swell; as a result of this the outer wall bursts and the inner walls, still enclosing the egg cells, lie free in the mucilage that fills the conceptacle, finally passing out through the ostiole, into the sea water.

Once outside the conceptacle, the double wall of the oögonium dissolves away, as also does the single wall of the antheridium, so that the egg cells and the sperms are liberated. The sperms swim towards the egg cells, attracted by a chemical substance that the egg cells give off. The sperms cluster round the egg cells, their eagerness causing the egg cells to spin round and round in the water. Eventually a sperm burrows into each egg cell, and fertilization is completed by the fusion of male and female nuclei.

After fertilization has been completed the fertilized egg cell grows a sticky cell wall which enables it to stick to any solid object with which it comes into contact. The act of becoming stuck appears to set up some sort of polarity in the fertile egg cell, for a cell wall is formed cutting off a cell at the end by which it is stuck; this cell later develops into the holdfast. The opposite end of the fertile egg grows out to form the stipe and the frond of the new plant.

We are not certain how this polarity in the fertilized egg cell is established, for to all appearances it is quite undifferentiated at this stage, and there is no obvious reason (apart from convenience) why the cell that becomes the holdfast should always develop at the point where the egg is attached to the substratum. Presumably some growth-regulating substance is formed in the protoplasm of the egg cell, and there is some evidence that this substance may be auxin, the common growth-regulating hormone found in all the higher plants. At any rate, the presence of auxin in the fertile eggs of *Fucus* has been experimentally demonstrated.

The polarity of the egg cell is not solely dependent on contact with a rock or other solid body, for it has been shown to be affected by other factors such as light, temperature, and the concentration of hydrogen ions in the water.

The bladder wrack commonly grows in the middle belt of the littoral or tidal zone on the shore. Higher up, near the high-tide mark, it tends to be replaced by a related species, the spiral wrack, *Fucus spiralis*, while lower down, towards the low-tide mark, we find the toothed wrack, *F. serratus*.

THE SPIRAL WRACK

The spiral wrack, *Fucus spiralis*, is a common seaweed occurring on rocks near the high-tide mark. It is olive-brown in colour, and is usually smaller than the bladder wrack, the fronds being normally from six to eighteen inches long. The branches of the frond are flat, with entire (i.e. not serrated or lobed) margins;

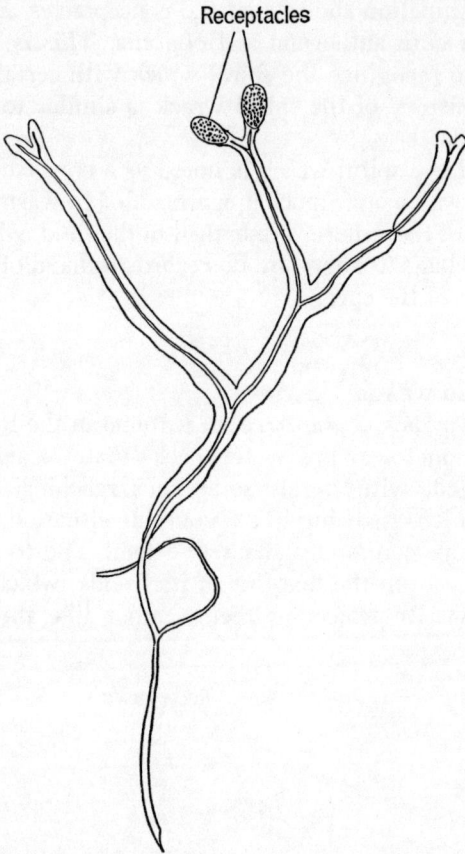

FIGURE 5.
Part of a frond of the spiral wrack (Fucus spiralis).

the tips of the branches are rounded. The fronds are often spirally twisted, hence the name of the seaweed (Fig. 5), but this is not a reliable character for the identification of the spiral wrack, for the twisting may not occur.

The tips of the branches of the fronds bear the receptacles, which are oval in outline and light brown in colour; when the plant is growing under good conditions it can often be recognized at a distance by its swollen, rounded receptacles. The spiral wrack has no air bladders.

If a section is cut of a receptacle of the spiral wrack, microscopical examination shows that the conceptacles are bisexual: they contain both antheridia and oögonia. This is, in fact, the safest way to recognize the spiral wrack with certainty.

The life history of the spiral wrack is similar to that of the bladder wrack.

In Ireland the spiral wrack is noted as a corn cure. The ripe receptacles, which ooze mucilage, are added to warm salt water, and the feet of the sufferer are bathed in the fluid, which is often called "jelly bags". There are no records to hand of the efficacy or otherwise of the cure.

THE TOOTHED WRACK

The toothed wrack, *Fucus serratus*, is found in the lower part of the littoral zone, near low-water mark (Plates 4 and 5). It is a large seaweed, with fronds sometimes reaching five feet in length when it is growing in a favourable situation, though the length is more commonly about two feet. The toothed wrack gets its name from the margins of its fronds, which notch into coarse, forwardly-projecting teeth, rather like the teeth of a saw (Fig. 6).

FIGURE 6.
Part of a frond of the toothed wrack (Fucus serratus).

Plate 1. The bladder wrack (*Fucus vesiculosus*) growing on rocks in the intertidal zone, Bembridge, Isle of Wight.

Plate 2. Photomicrograph of a section through a male conceptacle of the bladder wrack. The antheridia are visible as small, deeply-stained objects.

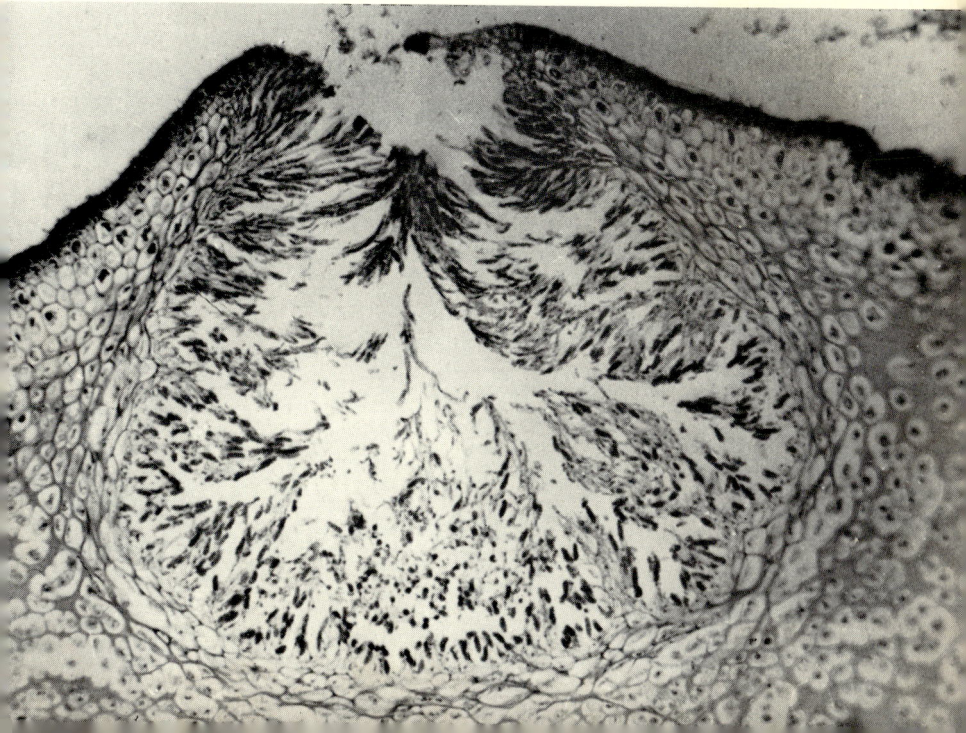

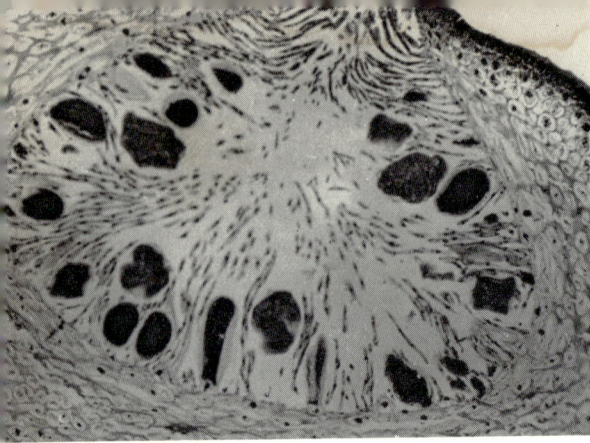

Plate 3. Photomicrograph of a section through a female conceptacle of the bladder wrack. The dark, more or less egg-shaped bodies are oögonia.

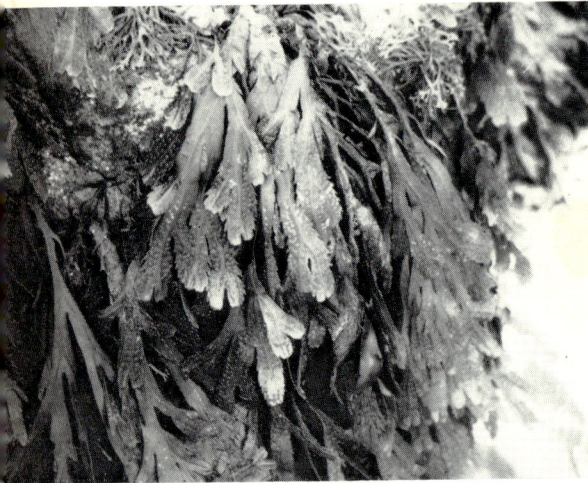

Plate 4. The toothed wrack (*Fucus serratus*) in close-up view, St. Briac, Brittany.

Plate 5. Rocks near low-tide mark covered with a good growth of the toothed wrack (*Fucus serratus*). In the middle foreground can be seen some specimens of the sea belt (*Laminaria saccharina*) Paignton, Devon.

The receptacles of the toothed wrack are less distinct from the rest of the fronds than they are in most species of *Fucus*. They are areas from one to two inches long, where the frond is lightly thickened. Male and female receptacles occur on different plants.

The toothed wrack is extremely widespread round British coasts, often forming a dense stand on the rocks near the low-tide mark. Its fronds lie flat against the rock, and often give shelter to marine invertebrates of various kinds. Zoophytes frequently occur beneath its shelter, and the marine worm *Spirorbis* often forms colonies which make a conspicuous pattern on its fronds.

THE HORNED WRACK

The horned wrack, *Fucus cerenoides*, is typical of brackish rather than fully salt water, and is usually found in estuaries where the sea water is diluted by water flowing out from a river. It may also occur in sheltered bays well surrounded by land. It is not found sharing the sea shore with the other three species of *Fucus*.

The horned wrack is a comparatively small plant, with fronds from nine to eighteen inches long. The fronds are rather narrow, with a conspicuous midrib from which the blade may get stripped, giving the impression of short branches attached to a long, branching stipe. It is fairly easily distinguished from other

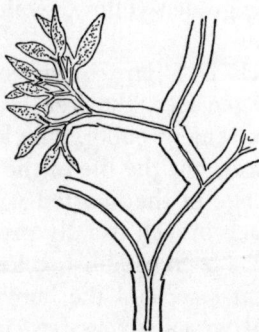

FIGURE 7.
Part of a frond of the horned wrack (Fucus ceranoides).

species of *Fucus* by its pale, olive-green colour, and by its branches, which tend to be somewhat fan-shaped and which end in long, pointed receptacles, from which this seaweed gets its name "horned wrack" (Fig. 7).

The horned wrack usually has its male and female sex organs on different plants, but occasionally they may occur on the same plant.

A fifth species of *Fucus*, *F. anceps*, is sometimes found growing in patches on ledges on the sides of rocks, It has a short stipe, and the frond measures only an inch or two in length, with a distinct midrib and no air bladders. It can be distinguished from the horned wrack by its small size, and by its receptacles, which end with a point of sterile tissue.

THE KNOTTED WRACK

The knotted wrack (*Ascophyllum nodosum*) is a common seaweed which usually occupies a band on the middle of the shore, above the bladder wrack, though it is sometimes found just below it. The genus *Ascophyllum* differs from *Fucus* in the absence of a midrib. Its fronds are narrow, with serrated margins, and they are swollen every two or three inches to form large air bladders (Fig. 8). The size of the air bladders varies, but in well-grown specimens of the knotted wrack they may be as large as walnuts. The receptacles are formed on short branches along the fronds. The sexes are found on different plants and the sex of a plant can be determined from the colour of the receptacles, those of the male plants being golden-yellow, while those of the female plants are olive-yellow.

The knotted wrack is a large seaweed, the fronds often reaching a length of ten feet, the free branching of the frond making the plants extremely bulky. The knotted wrack grows more slowly than *Fucus*, but the life of the plant is longer. One can tell roughly the age of the knotted wrack by counting the air bladders, since each branch usually produces one bladder a year after the plant has been established for a year or two.

Because of its great size, and the buoyancy of its large air bladders, the knotted wrack grows best on a gently shelving beach where it is not subjected to the full force of rough seas. It needs a firm substratum, such as a large rock or boulder, to

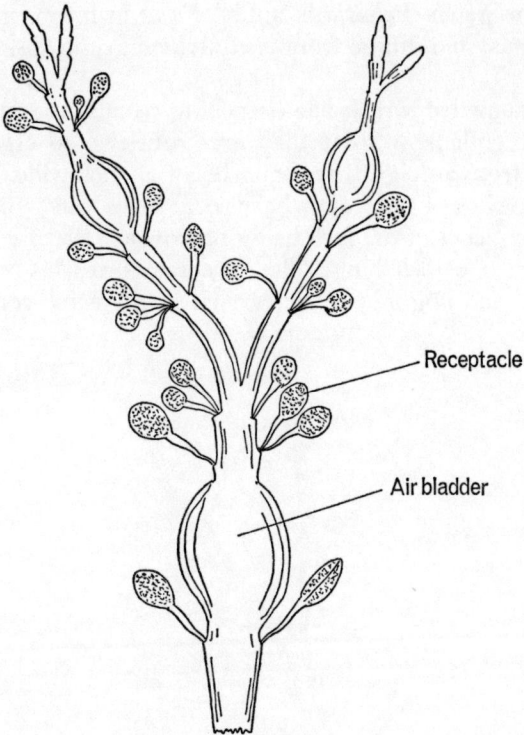

FIGURE 8.
Part of a frond of the knotted wrack (Ascophyllum nodosum).

which it can anchor itself by its holdfast. Where these conditions are fulfilled it can grow in large quantities, excluding other sea-weeds from the area it occupies.

The fronds of the knotted wrack sometimes bear rounded nodules projecting from the surface. These are galls, formed by the eelworm *Tylenchus fucicola* which parasitizes the knotted wrack and other seaweeds.

THE CHANNELLED WRACK

The channelled wrack, *Pelvetia canaliculata*, is another seaweed that is common on British shores, growing in tufts from extreme high-water mark, or sometimes even a little above it, down to the zone where the spiral wrack takes over dominance of the

shore. The genus *Pelvetia* is unlike *Fucus* in having no midrib
to its fronds, and differs from *Ascophyllum* in the absence of air
bladders.

The channelled wrack has branching fronds, the margins of
which are rolled inwards; they are from two to eight inches
long and from an eighth to a quarter of an inch wide. The ends
of the branches of the fronds bear receptacles which are forked,
the two branches of the fork being narrow and usually from half
an inch to one inch long. The receptacles are bisexual, both
antheridia and oögonia being carried in the same conceptacle.

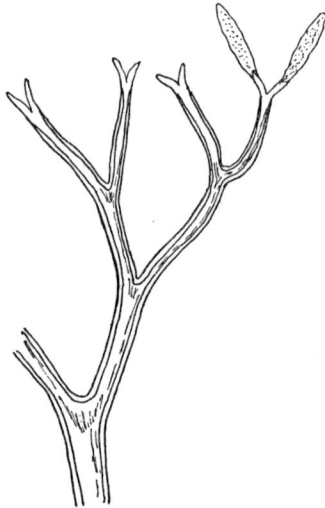

FIGURE 9.
Part of a frond of the channelled wrack (Pelvetia canaliculata).

When mature, the receptacles are yellowish-green in colour
(Fig. 9).

When the channelled wrack is uncovered by the tide—which
it is for most of the time—the fronds lie on the rocks with their
concave sides downwards. A certain amount of water is trapped
between the frond and the rock, and this enables the channelled
wrack to survive for considerable periods without immersion in
water. During the periods of spring tides most of the plants are
covered daily with water, but during the neap tide period they
may be uncovered for days at a time. The channelled wrack can

even grow above the high-tide mark, where it is never really covered at all, but merely washed by flung spray. Such plants are usually small.

The channelled wrack is used as fodder for sheep and cattle, particularly in Scotland. Owing to the readiness with which cattle, in particular, eat it in quantity it is sometimes called "cow tang" by the Scots.

THE SEA THONG

The sea thong, *Himanthalia elongata*, belongs to the family Himanthaliaceae, a family related to the Fucaceae. The sea thong has a most peculiar habit of growth, which makes it the easiest of all the seaweeds to identify.

A young plant of the sea thong consists of a small olive-brown object, at first club-shaped, but finally becoming flattened like a button, from one to two inches in diameter. From the middle of this button the fertile branches of the frond grow out to a length of from four to eight feet. The fertile branches are narrow and strap-like, and they fork several times in the course of their length (Fig. 10).

The fertile branches of the sea thong are yellowish in colour. When the conceptacles are ripe, which is during the spring and early summer, small brown spots appear on the fertile branches, each marking the opening leading to the cavity of a conceptacle. These spots may appear all over the surface of the branches, showing that the whole of the branch is fertile. If we compare the sea thong with a species of *Fucus* it would appear that the whole of the branch system of the sea thong corresponds with the receptacles of *Fucus*, the sterile part of the frond being the small button.

The male and female sex organs of the sea thong are on different plants. The whole of the strap-shaped fertile region (receptacle) dies away at the end of the growing season, new ones being formed the following year.

The sea thong grows in deep pools anywhere on the shore, or among rocks below the belt of serrated wrack. The yellow ochre of the fertile branches of the sea thong often stand out distinctly against the darker brown of the oarweeds growing at or below the low-tide mark.

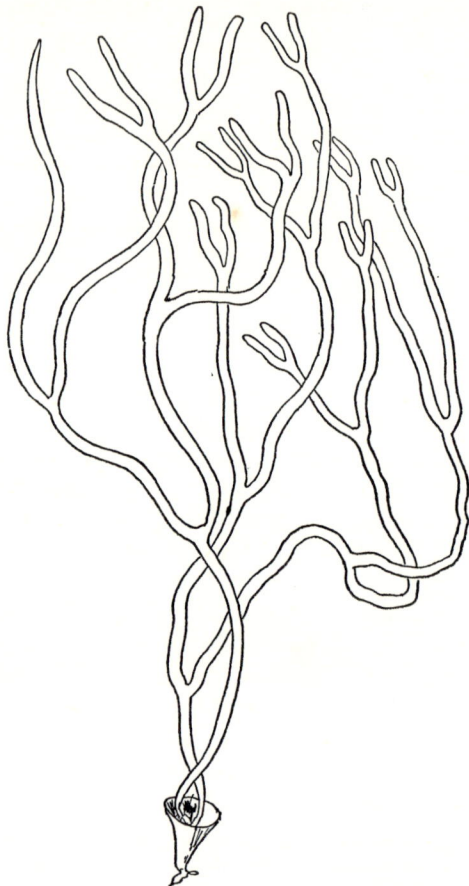

FIGURE 10.
The sea thong (Himanthalia elongata).

THE SEA OAK

The sea oak, *Halidrys siliquosa*, belongs to the Cytoseiraceae, a family of seaweeds living on the lower part of the beach, often beyond the low-tide mark. They may also inhabit some of the deeper pools. The family is common in the Mediterranean, where it replaces the wracks of the colder northern waters, but some, including the sea oak, are British.

The sea oak grows in deep rock pools, or below the low-tide mark, usually in positions where it gets some shelter from the

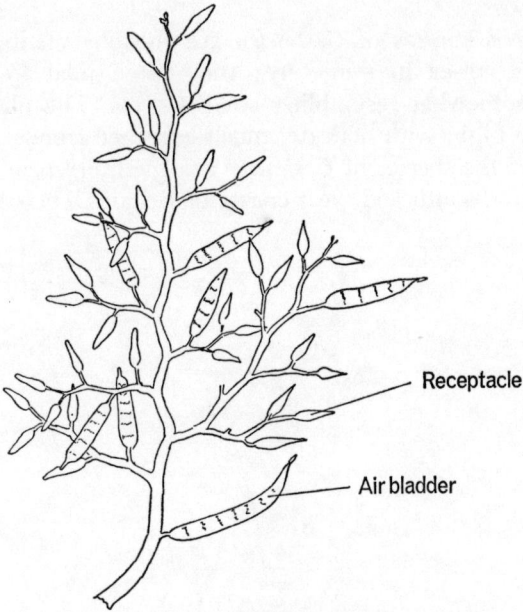

FIGURE 11.
The sea oak (Halidrys siliquosa).

full force of the elements. The fronds of the sea oak are from two to three feet long, and are attached to the rocks by a stout holdfast. The frond branches in a regular manner, forming a zig-zag which is easy to recognize (Plate 6 and Fig. 11). The branches of the frond bear air bladders of a characteristic shape, resembling the fruit, called a siliqua, typical of the cabbage family; it is because of this that it gets its specific epithet *siliquosa*. The bladders are anything from half an inch to two inches long, with pointed tips, and are divided crossways into from ten to twelve compartments by cross walls, the position of which can be seen by the transverse markings on the outer walls of the bladders.

We are uncertain how *Halidrys siliquosa* came to be called the sea oak, a name that is, in fact, a literal translation of the word *Halidrys*. Possibly the zig-zag branching of the frond was thought to be like the rather similar branching of an oak tree.

CYSTOSEIRA

The various species of *Cystoseira* are shrubby plants, looking rather like trees in miniature; they often tend to grow in colonies somewhat resembling small forests. The plants are a foot or so high, with delicate, much-branched fronds.

Most of the species of *Cystoseira* are Mediterranean, but four occur on the south and west coasts of Britain. The commonest

FIGURE 12.
Part of a frond of Cystoseira tamariscifolia.

British species are *C. tamariscifolia* and *C. fibrosa. C. tamariscifolia* has a much-branched frond a foot or so long which is covered with awl-shaped spines which look like leaves, about one-eighth of an inch in length (Fig. 12). The whole plant is densely shrubby and olive-brown in colour. When growing under water it shows iridescent colours which may or may not disappear when the plant is lifted into the air. The plant is easily recognized by its spiny branches, which give it a somewhat heather-like appearance. It was formerly called *C. ericoides*, from *Erica*, the botanical name for the heather.

C. fibrosa is a larger plant than *C. tamariscifolia*, usually reaching a height of two to three feet. The main branches lower down on the plant often lose their branchlets, but are covered with short stumps where the branchlets have broken off. The air bladders are large and conspicuous.

THE BULL WRACK

The bull wrack, or bull kelp, *Durvillea antarctica*, belongs to the family Durvilleaceae. It is the largest of the wracks, and inhabits sub-Antarctic seas in the region of New Zealand and the southern part of South America. In habit it resembles the kelps (see next

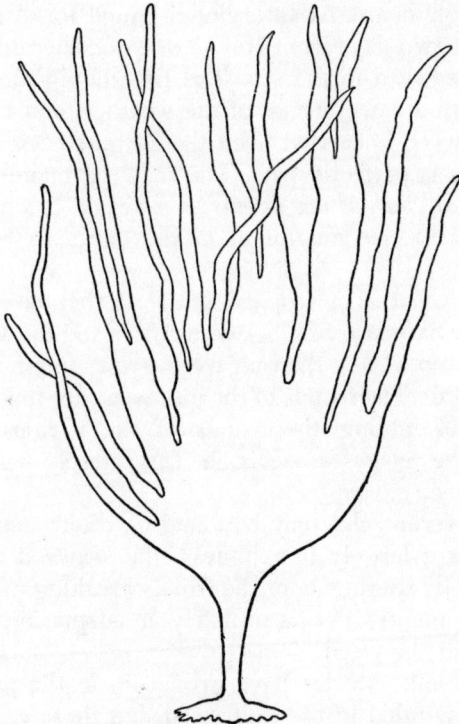

FIGURE 13.
The bull wrack (Durvillea).

chapter) rather than the wracks. It is provided with a massive holdfast which is often more than eighteen inches in diameter, and the enormous frond may be ten yards long. At first the frond consists of a massive, unbranched blade, but it later becomes split into many whip-like segments (Fig. 13). The stipe is short, but may reach a diameter of three inches.

The bull wrack usually grows in places where wave action is considerable, so that the plant is always covered with spray and so cannot dry out. Generally the holdfast is riddled with holes made by boring molluscs, and the bull wrack would soon lose moorings were it not for the fact that the holdfast forms new growth every year, a feature unusual in seaweeds.

THE GULF WEED

Passengers on board Atlantic liners bound for America often notice, about two days from New York, considerable quantities of floating seaweed in the sea. The time of sighting it usually coincides with a warming up of the weather, and they are told that the seaweed is carried from the Sargasso Sea by the Gulf Stream. This is perfectly true. The seaweed mainly consists of the gulf weed, *Sargassum natans*, a seaweed belonging to the family Sargassaceae and found in the Sargasso Sea in large quantities.

The gulf weed is a tropical seaweed that occurs in huge masses in the Sargasso Sea, between Africa and the West Indies. Unlike most seaweeds, the gulf weed grows unattached for the whole of its life. The fronds of the gulf weed are much branched, somewhat resembling the fronds of the various species of *Cystoseira*; the Sargassaceae is, in fact, closely related to the Cystoseiraceae.

Although receptacles may be found on the fronds of the gulf weed, they are largely functionless, the seaweed reproducing vegetatively by fragments of the fronds breaking off and growing into new plants, This is probably an adaptation to the free-floating life of the weed.

Many fearsome stories have grown up in the past of ships becoming entangled in the gulf weed, but these can all be put down to the vivid imaginations of sailors becalmed in the dreaded Sargasso Sea. Actually, the gulf weed is not all that large. There was once a theory that the gulf weed, with its entirely floating habit, was originally derived from the littoral seaweeds on the shores of the lost continent of Atlantis. Even if the fable of Atlantis were rooted in history, this is most unlikely.

The gulf weed is entirely tropical in its distribution, but occasionally the Gulf Stream carries a piece of it across the Atlantic and washes it up on the shores of Britain.

ZONATION OF THE WRACKS

Here and there in this chapter I have mentioned the occurrence of different species of wracks at certain levels on the shore. This phenomenon is called zonation, and it is best seen on a gently shelving, rocky beach with a reasonably large tide-fall. A northern latitude also favours zonation, for the brown seaweeds are more plentiful in cooler waters. Zonation is by no means confined to these places, however, for it can still be seen in Caribbean islands where the difference between high and low-tide marks is no more than nine inches.

On the cool Atlantic shores of Britain the highest zone is occupied by the channelled wrack, which may share this position with *Porphyra umbilicalis*, a common red seaweed. This belt is above the normal range of high tides, and is only covered by the highest of spring tides. Next, we have a belt of the spiral wrack, below that being a belt of the knotted wrack, followed by one of the bladder wrack; there is usually a middle belt between these last two where both the knotted wrack and the bladder wrack occur together. Finally, between the belt of bladder wrack and the low-tide mark, we get the toothed wrack.

The main factor in determining the position of these seaweed belts seems to be the length of time for which the various species can stand being emersed. Seaweeds such as the spiral wrack, and particularly the channelled wrack, can stand long periods of emersion; in fact, experiments have shown that they are killed if they are kept submerged all the time. At the other end of the scale, the toothed wrack cannot stand long periods of emersion, so that it grows only near to the low-tide mark, where it is covered with sea water for at least six hours out of every twelve.

In the sublittoral zone, below the low-tide mark, we find the oarweeds and kelps. In this zone they are never completely uncovered, except possibly for a few minutes by the lowest of spring tides. These seaweeds will be discussed in the next chapter.

WRACKS OF THE SALT-MARSHES

A salt-marsh is a coastal marshland where the water is salt. The marsh comes under the influence of the tides; the lower parts are covered at high tide, and the upper parts, which are above the normal high-tide level, are liable to flooding with sea water during the highest spring tides. Botanically, a salt-marsh is characterized by the presence of salt water, and by a high concentration of salt in the soil, and it bears a highly characteristic flora of halophytes (salt-loving plants). Most of these are seed plants, but some of the wracks may also play an important part in salt-marsh vegetation.

The wracks that occur on salt-marshes, especially at the higher levels, are most peculiar; there is evidently something about the salt-marsh habitat that completely alters the form of the seaweeds, so that it is difficult to recognize, say, the bladder wrack, in its salt-marsh form. As a group, the salt-marsh wracks possess certain characteristics which are not shown in any other habitat. Holdfasts are absent, the seaweeds lying

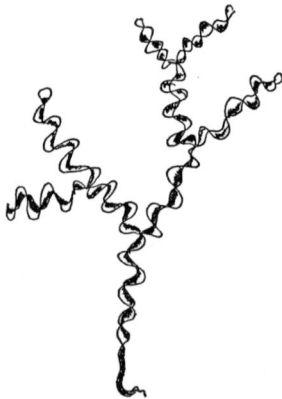

FIGURE 14.
Fucus vesiculosus *var.* volubilis, *a variety of the bladder wrack growing on salt marshes. Note the twisted frond.*

loose on the ground or in the water, depending on entanglement with other plants to keep them in place and prevent them from being washed away by the tide. The salt-marsh wracks are all dwarf in habit, and their fronds are spirally curved (Fig. 14). The sex organs are either absent altogether or do not function, the plants depending upon vegetative reproduction for their propagation; we have already noticed the same kind of thing in the gulf weed.

The salt-marsh wracks are best seen in East Anglia. In Norfolk, for instance, the salt-marsh form of the channelled wrack, and the three salt-marsh forms of the bladder wrack, may be found in profusion. Strangford Lough in Ireland, is also rich in salt-marsh forms of the wracks.

The salt-marsh wracks may play an important part in the initial colonization of salt-marshes by plants, their remains forming a kind of soil in which other plants can grow. They are also found growing among flowering plants in the higher parts of the salt-marsh, forming a layer covering the soil.

The kelps and oarweeds

We now come to the largest of the seaweeds: the giant kelps of the Pacific coast of America, and the smaller, but still sizeable, oarweeds that grow around our own coast.

The term "kelp" is rather vague. It may be applied to any large seaweed with a flattened frond belonging to the order Laminariales, an order containing four families: Chordaceae, Laminariaceae, Lessoniaceae, and Alariaceae. The oarweeds belong to the Laminariaceae, and as they are the most familiar members of the Laminariales we will start with them.

The oarweeds (genus *Laminaria*) are large seaweeds that grow in the sublittoral zone, from just below low-tide mark down to a depth of about fifteen feet. The oarweeds are perennial plants, and the new growth takes place not at the tip of the frond but in the region between the frond and the stipe. The young fronds grow rapidly during the spring, pushing the old fronds away from the stipe until they finally drop off. Portions of the old fronds of the oarweeds are often washed up by autumn storms, and are sometimes known as "mayweed".

The oarweeds are provided with long, well-developed stipes, and the holdfast is also large, consisting of a number of short, stout, branched processes capable of clinging tightly to the rock on which the seaweed is growing.

The oarweeds have a varied history of usefulness, first in the old kelp burning industry for the production of soda, potash, and iodine, and later as a source of alginic acid and alginates. This has led to their being known by many local names, such as "cow's tail", a name that doubtless refers to the long, flexible stipe with its tufted end. The stipes, when separated from the frond, are sometimes called "slack marrows", a name that actually means "sea club", and refers to their former use as cudgels during brawls between kelp burners.

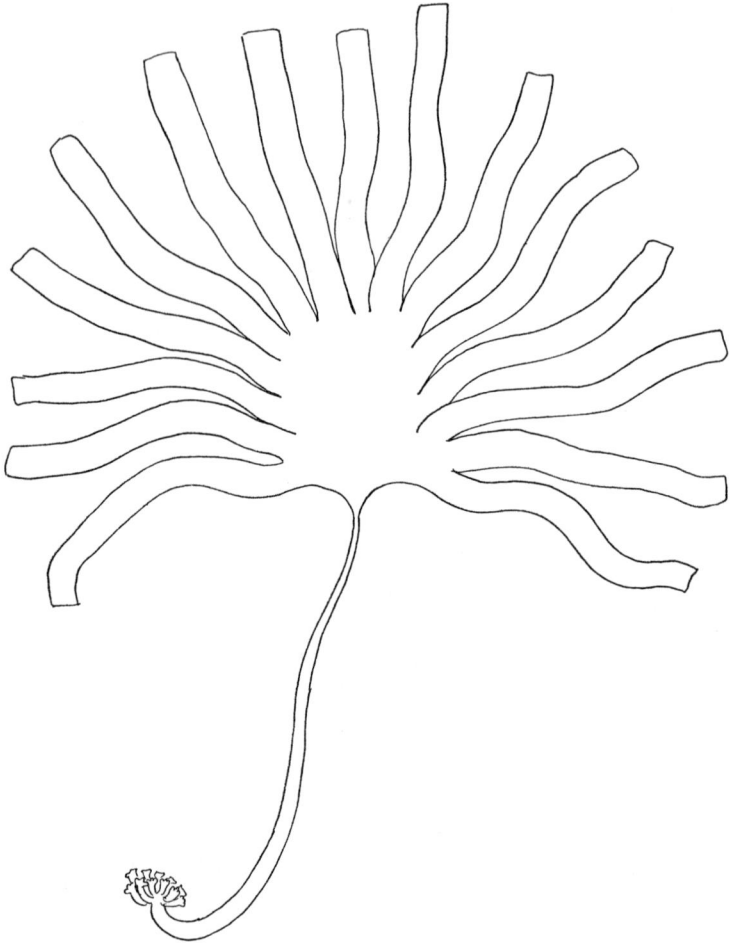

FIGURE 15.
The tangle (Laminaria digitata).

THE TANGLE

The tangle, *Laminaria digitata,* is a common seaweed that occurs in the upper limit of the sublittoral zone, just below low tide mark. It is a large seaweed, with a long flexible stipe and a flat, leathery frond which is narrow when first formed, but which increases in width with age until it becomes fan-shaped and two feet or more in diameter. As it increases in width the frond splits into strap-shaped segments, like the fingers of a hand (Fig. 15). The width of the segments varies according to the amount of wave action to which the frond is exposed; in sheltered situations the segments are few and wide, while in more exposed places they are many and narrow.

In early spring new growth appears at the base of the frond, forming the new season's blade. The newly-grown frond is light brown in colour, as opposed to the dark brown of the old frond, which remains attached as the new frond grows until constant wear causes the old frond to fall off. Old fronds thrown up on the beach by the waves soon become green as rain washes out the brown fucoxanthin, leaving the green of the chlorophyll exposed. Later, they are bleached nearly white.

The microscopic structure of the tangle is even more complex than that of the bladder wrack; the Laminariales, as befits their large size, are more advanced in structure than any other group of seaweeds. The stipe is divided into three regions. On the outside there is an epidermis, a layer of cells that forms a continuous covering over the whole plant. The epidermis may be one or two cells thick. Inside it is the cortex, a region where the cells are tightly packed together.

The innermost region is the medulla, which consists of unbranched filaments of cells running lengthways, connected by shorter filaments that run crossways. Of the filaments that run

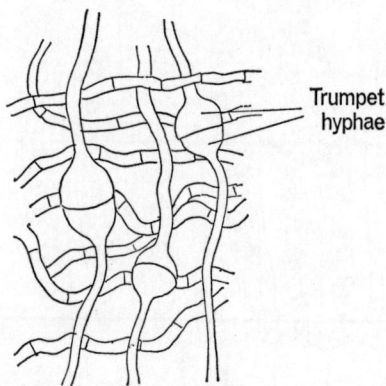

Trumpet hyphae

FIGURE 16.
Part of the developing cortex of the tangle, showing the trumpet hyphae.

longitudinally, several different kinds can be distinguished. Some under-go cell division as they lengthen, so that the filaments come to be composed of numerous, rather short cells. Other filaments divide only occasionally, so that the cells of which they are composed remain long. The ends of these filaments are expanded in a trumpet-like manner; they are known as trumpet hyphae (Fig. 16). It is believed that the trumpet hyphae serve to conduct elaborated food material away from the photosynthesizing cells to the parts of the plant where it is needed, just as the sieve tubes of higher plants conduct food that has been manufactured in the leaves. In some kelps, particularly *Macrocystis* and *Nereocystis*, the trumpet hyphae are provided with perforated end walls, like the sieve plates in the sieve tubes of higher plants.

The frond has much the same structure as the stipe. There is an epidermis which is one cell thick, a cortex, and a medulla of longitudinal filaments connected by filaments running crossways. The cells of the epidermis, and those of the outer layers of the cortex, contain chloroplasts, and it is here that photosynthesis takes place.

The reproductive cycle of the tangle is more complex than

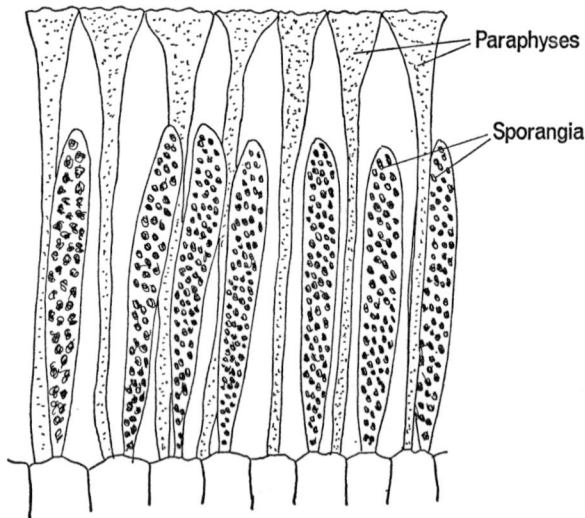

FIGURE 17.
Part of a sorus of Laminaria, *greatly magnified*

that of the bladder wrack, for there are two distinct methods of reproduction. One is a sexual process, involving the fertilization of an egg cell by a sperm as in the bladder wrack, while the other depends on the production of minute reproductive bodies called spores; as no sexual process is involved, this is known as asexual reproduction. Asexual reproduction by means of spores should not be confused with vegetative production in which spores are not formed.

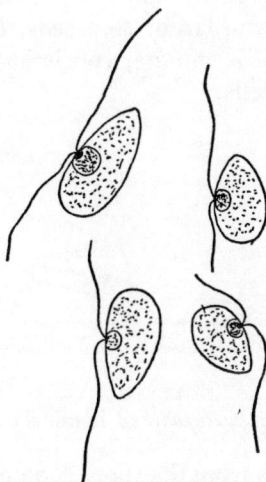

FIGURE 18.
Zoöspores of Laminaria

The spores of the tangle are produced in cells called sporangia, which are formed in groups called sori all over the surface of the frond (Plate 7 and Fig. 17). The sporangia are formed from epidermal cells, and their formation is preceded by the growth of a dense covering of hairs, called paraphyses, among which the sporangia are found.

At first a sporangium contains one nucleus, but this divides several times, forming either thirty-two or sixty-four nuclei. Some protoplasm gathers round each nucleus, the whole forming a spore. The spores are then liberated by the bursting open of the sporangium, and find themselves at large in the sea.

A spore of the tangle consists of a minute cell, invisible to the naked eye, oval in outline, with bluntly pointed ends. At one side there are inserted a pair of flagella: whip-like protoplasmic processes by the beating of which the spore are able to swim (Fig. 18). Because of their animal-like power of mobility the spores are known as zoöspores. They may also be called swarm spores, because of their habit of swimming around, or "swarming", after liberation.

The zoöspore of the tangle gives rise to a new plant, usually on a submerged rock or stone. This plant, however, is entirely different from the seaweed we know as the tangle. The original tangle plant is one of the larger seaweeds, but the new plant derived from the spore is minute, consisting of a microscopic filament of only a few cells.

FIGURE 19.
Male gametophyte of Laminaria.

The plant that grows from the spore soon produces reproductive organs, reproduction this time being sexual. The little plants are of two kinds: male and female. The male plant forms short lateral branches of one or two cells, and on these the antheridia are formed (Fig. 19). The antheridium consists of one small cell, which produces a single sperm. The female plant is even smaller than the male plant. Any of the few cells of which it is composed is potentially capable of becoming an oogonium (Fig. 20), containing a single egg cell which, when ripe, is extruded through a pore in the top of the oogonium, where it remains attached. The egg cell is fertilized by a wandering sperm, and from the fertile egg a new plant grows: this time a large plant of the kind we recognize as the tangle.

From this we can see that the life history of the tangle consists of two generations, a different type of plant occurring in each. The large plant bears the sporangia and spores, so it is called

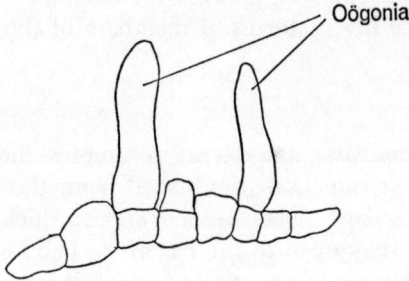

FIGURE 20.
Female gametophyte of Laminaria.

the sporophyte. The small plant bears the sex organs which produce the sex cells or gametes; it is therefore called the gametophyte. The spores always give rise to the gametophyte generation, never another sporophyte, and similarly the fertilized egg, product of the gametophyte generation, always produces a sporophyte and never another gametophyte. There is thus a regular alternation of generations, the sporophyte being followed by the gametophyte, which in turn is followed by another sporophyte.

Alternation of generations is an extremely common phenomenon in the algae, and we shall meet it again and again. In the tangle the two generations are entirely dissimilar in form, and for this reason the alternation of generations is said to be heteromorphic. This is not always the case, for in some seaweeds the two generations are alike in everything except the kind of reproductive organs they bear; in a case like this the alternation of generations is said to be isomorphic.

Alternation of generations is by no means confined to the seaweeds; in fact, *all* plants above the algae and fungi in the evolutionary scale show the phenomenon. In the flowering plants, for instance, the plant that we see and know is the sporophyte. The gametophyte is so reduced that it consists only of the pollen grain and its product, the pollen tube, and a cell called the embryo sac which is hidden away in the ovule or immature seed. Alternation of generations in the flowering plant, therefore, is highly heteromorphic.

The heteromorphic alternation of generations of the tangle,

with the large and imposing sporophyte and minute gametophyte, is typical of the life histories of members of the Laminariales.

THE CUVIE

The cuvie (*Laminaria hyperborea*) resembles the tangle in its general habit. It can be distinguished from the tangle by the presence of mucilage ducts on the stipe, which form minute pimples where they open to the exterior. The holdfast is more conical, the branches of the stipe of which it is composed being formed in vertical rows, giving it greater depth. The stipe of the cuvie is broader at the base than that of the tangle, and the stipe as a whole is more rigid (Fig. 21). Otherwise, the cuvie is very like the tangle, and at one time the two seaweeds were regarded as the same species.

The presence of mucilage makes the stipe of the cuvie somewhat sticky, with a result that it becomes the resting place for a large number of epiphytes (plants that live perched on other plants without being parasitic on them). The stipes of the cuvie often bear seaweeds such as *Rhodymenia palmata* and *Lomentaria articulata*, as well as various members of the Delessariaceae, all red seaweeds; they are also good hunting grounds for many of the smaller algae. One can usually tell the cuvie from the tangle by the number of epiphytes alone.

The cuvie tends to grow at slightly greater depths below

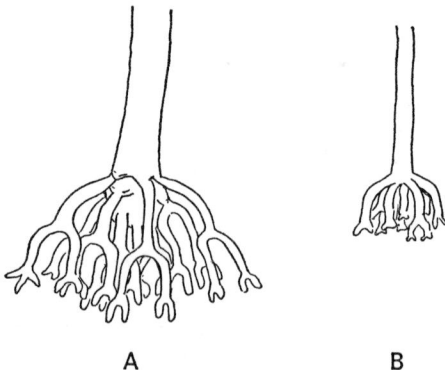

A   B

FIGURE 21.
Holdfasts of A, the cuvie and B, the tangle, drawn approximately to the same scale

the low-tide mark than the tangle, and continues down to a depth of about ninety feet. It is seldom uncovered except by the lowest of spring tides; on the rare occasions when this happens the plants stand erect, supported by their stiff stipes, with their fronds trailing in the water.

The stipes of the cuvie are a most useful source of alginic acid. After cutting off the fronds, the stipes are stacked to dry out before being transported to the alginate factories. Near the main collecting grounds there are often hundreds of tons stacked and awaiting transport.

The cuvie was formerly called *Laminaria cloustoni.*

THE SEA BELT

The sea belt, *Laminaria saccharina*, has quite a different habit from the cuvie (Plate 8). There is a branched holdfast and a flexible stipe, but the frond, instead of being expanded, is in the form of a ribbon, about six inches wide and five feet or so long. The central part of the frond is slightly thickened, and the edges are curled to form frills running the length of the frond (Fig. 22). The sporangia are carried on the thickened central stipe, sunken below its surface.

When dried, the fronds become coated with a sweet, white substance, the flavour of which is much appreciated by horses. This has earned the sea belt the popular name "sugar wrack" in some parts of the country. Strictly speaking the name "wrack" should not be applied to a seaweed belonging to the Laminariales, which are more properly called "kelps". The sea belt is known sometimes as the "poor man's weather glass" because its fronds may be hung on the wall to act as a rudimentary barometer: the frond is brittle to the touch in dry weather, becoming soft if wet weather is in the offing. It is not very reliable.

The sea belt is common round the shores of Britain, usually growing in fairly sheltered situations, It often occurs in deep rock pools, and on the shore from low-tide mark down to a depth of twenty feet or more.

Laminaria hieroglyphica is a seaweed closely allied to the sea belt, of which it is regarded by some authorities as a variety. It is a somewhat smaller seaweed than the sea belt, and is widespread on the coast of north-east Scotland.

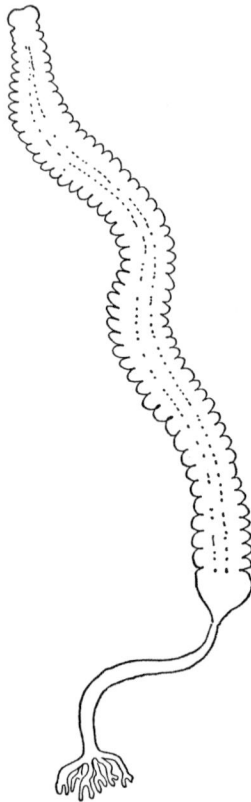

FIGURE 22.
The sea belt (Laminaria saccharina).

THE FURBELOWS

The furbelows, *Sacchoriza polyschides*, is the largest of seaweeds found on British coasts, the plants sometimes growing as long as fifteen feet and measuring twelve feet in breadth across the frond. The holdfast is at first a small disk, but later in the growing season a bulbous structure arises on the stipe, just above the holdfast, and from the bulb a number of descending branches develop which eventually take the place of the original holdfast.

The stipe of the furbelows is flattened, and its margins are frilled. At the end of the stipe the large frond is formed; this is semi-circular and split into a number of strap-like segments (Fig. 23).

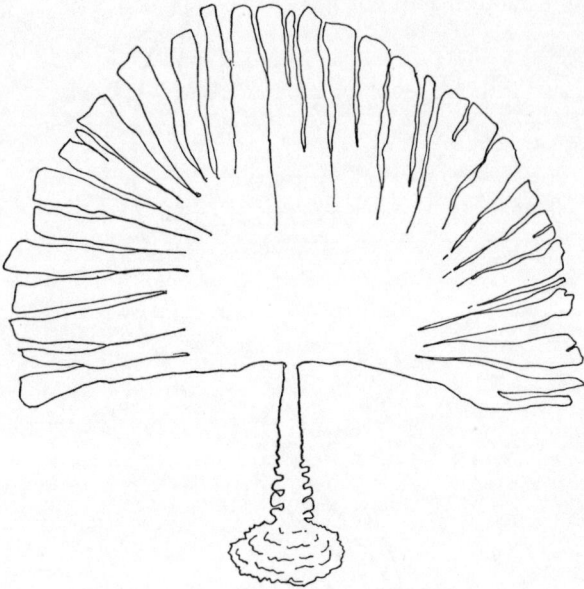

FIGURE 23.
The furbelows (Sacchoriza polyschides).

In spite of its excessive size, the furbelows is an annual plant, completing its growth in one season.

The furbelows grows from just below low water mark down to a depth of about 100 feet, its size increasing with depth. It is usually placed in the Laminariaceae by British algologists, but some authorities place it in a separate family called the Phyllariaceae. A second species of *Sacchoriza*, *S. dermatodea*, occurs in Polar seas.

THE DABBERLOCKS

The dabberlocks, *Alaria esculenta*, belongs to the family Alariaceae. It differs from members of the Laminariaceae by the fact that its frond possesses a midrib, and also by having special reproductive "leaves" which bear the sporangia.

The dabberlocks has the usual branched holdfast, and a short stipe, not more than six inches long. Above the stipe is the long, narrow frond, which is from two to twenty feet long and from

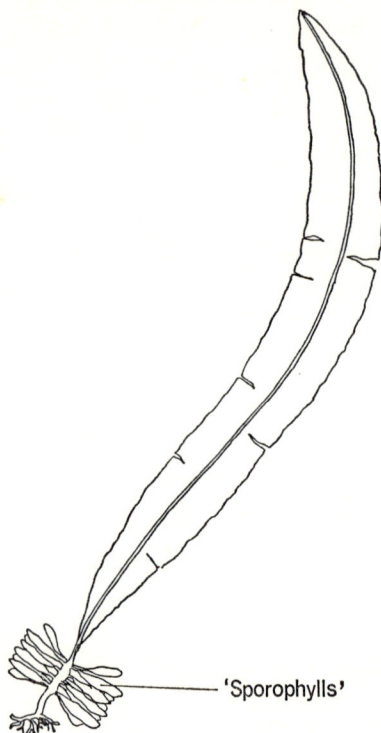

'Sporophylls'

FIGURE 24.
The dabberlocks (Alaria esculenta).

two to six inches wide. From the stipe, just below the frond, the reproductive blades, or "sporophylls", are given off; these are lance-shaped or oval, and the sporangia are embedded in them, the frond itself being sterile. The edges of the frond are somewhat curled (Fig. 24).

The dabberlocks is a common seaweed round the northern coasts of Britain, but it is rare in the south. It likes a cool climate, and usually reaches its best development during the winter. In Scotland and Ireland the fleshy midribs are eaten, a habit that has been going on for some time, for Turner, in his *Historia fucorum*, published in 1809, mentions the eating of the midrib of a seaweed which "goes by the name of Daberlocks".

The dabberlocks is found growing on rocks just below the low-tide mark. It is always submerged.

THE SEA LACE

The sea lace, *Chorda filum*, belongs to the family Chordaceae. Although it does not differ from the kelps we have considered in any vital point, its general habit is very different from that of any other member of the Laminariales. There is a small hold-fast, from which arises a cylindrical frond which may reach a length of twenty-five feet, although its diameter is nowhere greater than a quarter of an inch. It has the appearance of a thick bootlace growing in the water (Fig. 25), an appearance that is

FIGURE 25.
The sea lace (Chorda filum).

reflected in its name. The frond is hollow throughout except for diaphragms which cross it here and there.

In the details of its life history the sea lace follows the general pattern shown by the oarweeds and other Laminariales.

The sea lace occurs all over the cooler parts of the northern hemisphere; it is extremely abundant, especially in more sheltered waters, growing from low-tide mark down to a depth of sixty feet or so. The plants often grow in great masses, and can entangle a swimmer who is foolish enough to attempt to swim through them; hence their alternative popular name, "dead men's ropes". They are also occasionally known as "mermaid's tresses" and "cat gut".

THE GIANT KELPS

The giant kelps are the largest of the seaweeds. They belong to the family Lessoniaceae, and are to be found in the cooler parts of the Pacific Ocean.

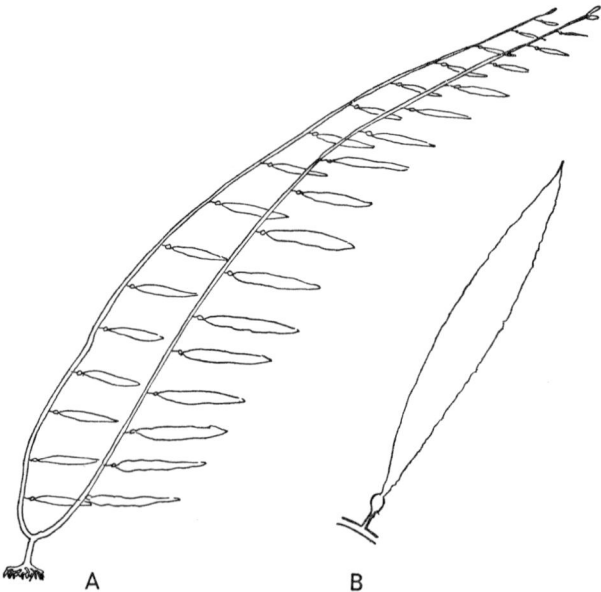

FIGURE 26.
The giant kelp (Macrocystis pyrifera). *A, habit; B, detail of frond.*

The largest of the giant kelps is *Macrocystis*, a gigantic sea-weed living at depths of from 60 to 90 feet in the North and South Pacific, and near the Cape of Good Hope. The temperature of the water in the areas occupied by *Macrocystis* varies between 0° and 20°C. *M. pyrifera* is the largest and best-known species.

Macrocystis is anchored to the sea bottom by a massive holdfast, which may be a yard or more in diameter. From the holdfast arises a thick, short primary stipe, which soon branches to form several long secondary stipes bearing many leaf-like blades; these are lance-shaped, and from three to five feet long. At the base of each blade is a spherical or pear-shaped air bladder which provides buoyancy (Fig. 26). The blades,

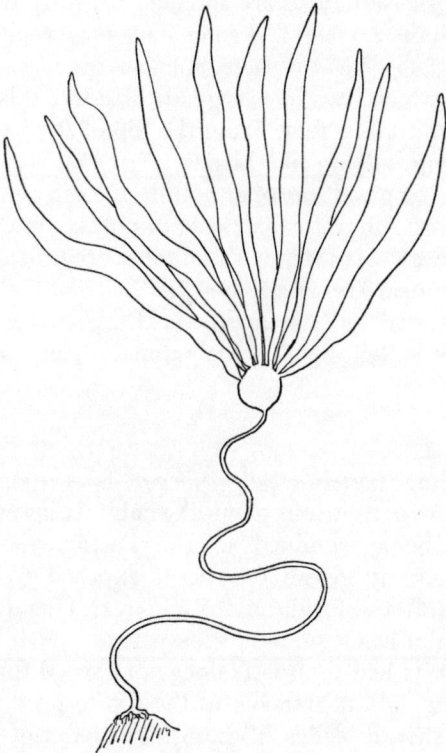

FIGURE 27.
Nereocystis luetkiana.

supported by the air bladders, float on the surface of the water, and the length of a single frond may be as much as 200 feet.

The sporangia of *Macrocystis* are carried on special, smaller fronds which arise near the base of the stipe. These remain comparatively short and do not reach the surface of the water.

Macrocystis is of considerable economic importance as a source of alginic acid. In California it is the only seaweed used for this purpose, the fronds being cut by means of a mechanical harvester mounted in a harvesting barge.

Nereocystis is another gigantic seaweed which grows at a depth of from fifteen to seventy-five feet between Alaska and Los Angeles. Locally it is known by a variety of names, including "bull kelp", "bladder kelp", "ribbon kelp", and "sea-otters' cabbage" (Plate 9).

The plants of *Nereocystis* are annuals, but in spite of this they reach a length of 150 feet, and some have been reported to be as long as 270 feet. The massive holdfast gives rise to a long slender stipe which ends in a large air bladder; this may have a diameter of up to nine feet. From the top of the baldder arise a number of long, ribbon-like blades (Fig. 27).

Nereocystis is a good source of potash, the ash containing from twenty-seven to thirty-five per cent of potassium chloride. The stipe and the air bladder, with suitable treatment, provide a candied sweetmeat known as "Seatron".

Closely related to *Nereocystis* is *Pelagophycus*, a seaweed known locally as "elk-kelp", "sea pumpkin", and "sea orange".

THE SEA PALM

The sea palm, *Postelsia palmaeformis* is a member of the Lessoniaceae with a curious palm-like habit. It is restricted in its distribution, being confined to the Pacific coast of North America, where it grows on rocks, exposed to heavy surf, between central California and Vancouver Island.

The sea palm has a smooth, glossy stipe which is extremely thick, though its length usually does not exceed three feet. The stipe is hollow, and it branches at the top to produce from 100 to 150 strap-shaped blades (Fig. 28). The habit of the sea palm strongly reminds one of a palm tree, and the resemblance is particularly striking when a forest of sea palms growing on a

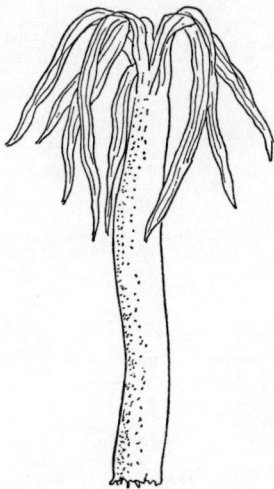

FIGURE 28.
Young plant of the sea palm (Postelsia palmaeformis).

rocky headland is uncovered at low tide, and stands resisting the efforts of the heavy surf to dislodge it.

Somewhat resembling the sea palm is *Lessonia flavicans*, a seaweed that grows in deep water off the shores of the South Pacific, forming submarine forests that resemble the extinct swamp forests of Carboniferous times (Fig. 29).

Lessonia flavicans has a rigid stipe from five to ten feet long and about nine inches thick. It is branched near its top, and the branches bear a number of drooping blades which look like leaves. The sporangia are formed on the lower parts of the blades. The whole plant may reach a height of twelve feet.

SEAWEEDS AND PHOTOSYNTHESIS

The Laminariales are all seaweeds of the sublittoral zone, or of deep water; at most, some species are uncovered for a short time at low tide. This means that light has to travel through a varying amount of water before it reaches them. Water, although transparent, has nevertheless got considerable stopping power for light, so that it is always a problem for a submerged plant to get enough light for adequate photosynthesis. This factor is complicated by the fact that light travelling through

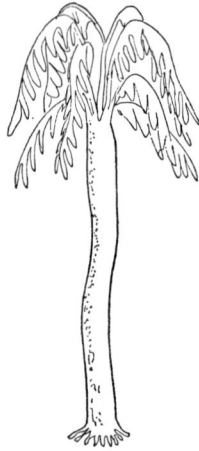

FIGURE 29.
Lessonia flavicans.

water is green, the water tending to filter out the other colours. For a normal green plant, green is the worst colour for light to have if it is to be used for photosynthesis.

This can be seen if we examine a solution of chlorophyll by means of a spectroscope—an instrument which splits white light up into its component colours. If we examine the spectrum of light which has passed through a chlorophyll solution we can see that much of the red-orange and blue-violet ends of the spectrum are blotted out, while the green light comes through. This means that the chlorophyll is absorbing the red-orange and blue-violet light strongly, but allowing the green to pass. It follows, therefore, that the chlorophyll is using the red-orange and blue-violet light for photosynthesis, but making little use of the green, which is allowed to pass through. This is confirmed by experiment.

There is also the turbidity of the water to be considered. The more turbid the water is, owing to the presence of fine particles of sediment, or to the vigorous growth of microscopic organisms of the plankton, the less light it is able to transmit. This will have its effect on the growth of seaweeds. In the muddy waters of the Atlantic seaweeds seldom grow at a depth greater than 100 feet, whereas in the clear water of the Mediterranean they can grow at much greater depths. In the Bay of Naples, for

Plate 6. The sea oak (*Halidrys siliquosa*), Charmouth, Dorset.

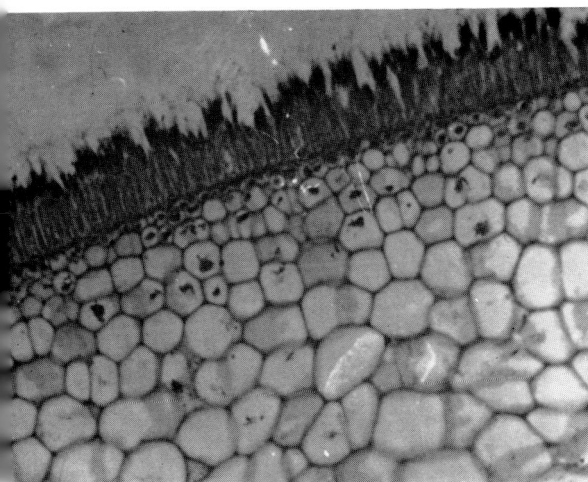

Plate 7. Photomicrograph of part of the blade of *Laminaria*, showing the sporangia.

Plate 8. The sea belt (*Laminaria saccharina*) growing at low-tide mark, Paignton, Devon.

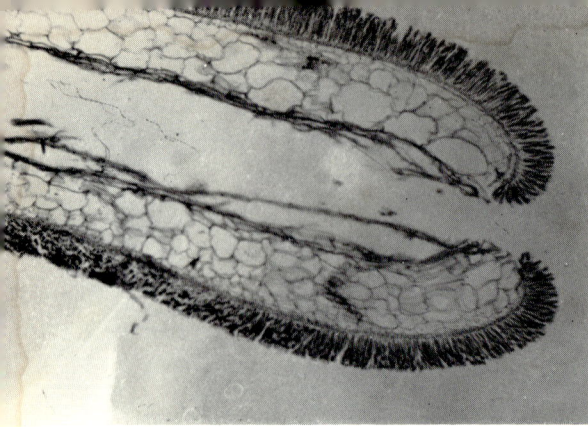

Plate 9. Photomicrograph of part of the frond of *Nereocystis*, showing the sporangia.

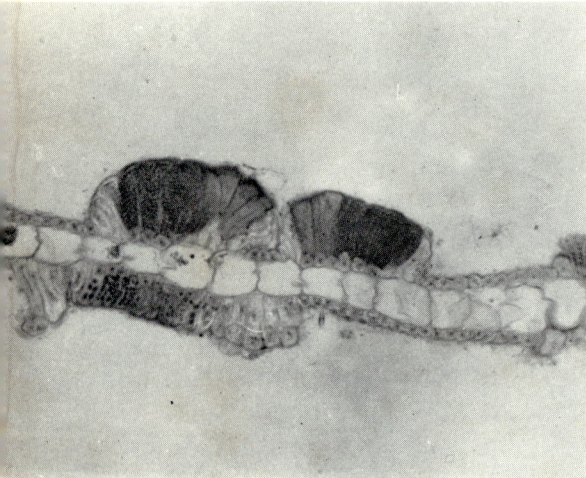

Plate 10. Photomicrograph of part of the frond of *Dictyota dichotoma*, showing sori of antheridia.

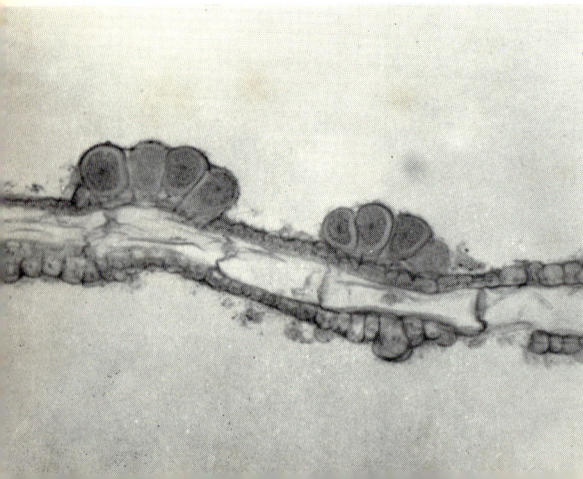

Plate 11. Photomicrograph of part of the frond of *Dictyota dichotoma*, showing oögonial sori.

instance, they grow down to 400 feet, and off the Balearic Islands they have been found at a depth of over 500 feet. While the effect of the stronger sunlight in the Mediterranean should not be minimized, the much clearer water—the Mediterranean is sterile compared with the Atlantic—also has its effect.

From all this it might seem as though the photosynthetic prospects for seaweeds were fairly poor, but living organisms have a habit of adapting to circumstances in a manner that smacks of the miraculous. There are several ways in which the seaweeds are adapted to carry out photosynthesis in the light available to them.

Firstly, for every plant, whether it be a land plant or a sea-weed, there is an optimum light intensity at which photosynthesis is most efficient. Determination of this optimum light intensity for the seaweeds has shown the interesting fact that for a littoral seaweed such as the bladder wrack, which is exposed for a considerable part of its life, the optimum light for photosynthesis is about the same for an average land plant, whereas for a sublittoral species such as the tangle, which is virtually always covered by the tide, the optimum light intensity is lower. In other words, a sublittoral seaweed not only does not need strong light for photosynthesis: it actually prefers the dusk of the ocean.

This adaptation becomes even more obvious when we examine some of the giant seaweeds that grow in relatively deep water. For *Macrocystis*, and for the allied genus *Egregia*, which belongs to the Alariaceae, it has been shown that the optimum light intensity for photosynthesis varies in different parts of the same plant, becoming lower as we pass down the plant into deeper water.

Allied to the optimum light intensity for photosynthesis is the compensation point. This is the point where photosynthesis just balances respiration. By photosynthesis plants use carbon dioxide with water to form sugar, giving off oxygen. Plants, however, also respire, just as animals do, and in respiration they oxidize sugar to form carbon dioxide and water, which is the opposite of photosynthesis. During daylight both processes are going on simultaneously, but as photosynthesis is greatly in excess of respiration, the respiratory process is masked. As the light gets dimmer, photosynthesis becomes less until it

3

finally ceases, but respiration, not being dependent on light, goes on. It follows, therefore, that there must be a light intensity at which photosynthesis just balances respiration. At this point the plant will appear to be neither photosynthesizing nor respiring, though actually each is going on at an equal rate, as can be shown by laboratory experiments. This is the compensation point.

For a submerged seaweed, the compensation point is low compared with that of a land plant. This is what we might expect from the low optimum intensity of light for photosynthesis that is found in sublittoral seaweeds.

Chromatic adaptation

By chromatic adaptation we mean the development in the chloroplast of accessory pigments with colours complementary to that of chlorophyll, so that light that is not absorbed by chlorophyll can be absorbed by them and used for photosynthesis.

In the higher plants the chloroplasts contain four pigments: chlorophyll *a*, chlorophyll *b*, xanthophyll, and carotene. The terms xanthophyll and carotene are really collective, for there are at least seventeen different xanthophylls, all with the same chemical formula but with slightly different properties, and, similarly, there are at least four different carotenes, again with the same chemical formula. The chloroplasts of any given species do not contain all the different xanthophylls and carotenes.

The main work of photosynthesis is carried out only by chlorophyll *a*, but there is evidence that the other pigments can assist with the process. When chlorophyll absorbs light of certain wavelengths it becomes excited: that is, the electrons in the atoms of its molecules jump into higher orbits as a result of the light energy that has been absorbed. Presently the electrons drop back into their former orbits, and the energy is given out again. The peculiar property that makes chlorophyll *a* so valuable is that the energy emitted by its molecules can be made to do chemical work: in other words, it can be used for photosynthesis.

That chlorophyll *a* is photochemically active is shown by its fluorescence. When it is illuminated with light of a suitable wavelength (colour) it glows. You can see the same sort of thing every time you switch on a television set, for the surface of the cathode-ray tube is coated with a substance which glows when struck by cathode rays.

The other pigments in the chloroplast do not play any direct part in photosynthesis. Like chlorophyll *a*, they are photochemically active: they can absorb light energy and give it out again. The energy that they give out is not used directly in photosynthesis, but it is absorbed by the chlorophyll *a* which can then use it for photosynthesis.

An elegant demonstration of this energy transference can be carried out in the laboratory if a mixture of chlorophyll and xanthophyll in a suitable solvent is illuminated by light of a wavelength that is absorbed by xanthophyll but not by chlorophyll. When this is done the chlorophyll becomes fluorescent, glowing with a beautiful deep red light. This could only happen if the chlorophyll molecules became excited by energy absorbed by the xanthophyll and passed on to them.

Turning now to the seaweeds, we find things even more complex. This is only to be expected, for the seaweeds have to make what use they can of light which is poor in intensity, besides being of an unsuitable colour. It is not surprising, therefore, to find in the seaweeds an abundance of pigments of a great variety of colours. Besides various chlorophylls in addition to chlorophyll *a* and chlorophyll *b* we find the red pigment phycoerythrin, the blue pigment phycocyanin, and the brown pigment fucoxanthin, all of which are photochemically active. There is no lack of pigments from which a seaweed can select a mixture to suit its needs.

The green seaweeds (Chlorophyta) contain the same mixture of pigments as the higher plants: chlorophyll *a*, chlorophyll *b*, xanthophyll, and carotene. They are the conservatives among the seaweeds. The rest contain a selection from the other pigments, as well as chlorophyll *a*, though not necessarily chlorophyll *b*.

Most interesting from the point of view of chromatic adaptation are the red seaweeds, whose chromatophores contain phycoerythrin and phycocyanin. Their colour can be anything from red to blue, but most of them show varying amounts of pink or red in their coloration. Since red is the complementary colour to green, we would expect the red seaweeds to be the best adapted for photosynthesizing in green light, the colour of sea water. We should therefore expect to find red algae growing at the greatest depths that seaweeds can attain.

This is, in fact, the case. Red seaweeds have been found at a depth of 600 feet, and no seaweed can grow deeper than this, owing to the darkness that extends beyond. This would seem to be a strong argument in favour of the existence of chromatic adaptation, were it not for one unfortunate fact. Green seaweeds have been found growing every bit as deep as red seaweeds!

What are we to conclude from this? Not, I think, that the whole idea of chromatic adaptation is a lot of arrant nonsense, for this would be throwing the baby out with the bath water. Laboratory tests have shown that fucoxanthin, phycoerythrin, and phycocyanin are capable of absorbing light and passing it on to chlorophyll *a*, which can then, presumably, use it for photosynthesis. There can be little doubt that chromatic adaptation works in Nature. What is in doubt is whether it is really necessary. Perhaps it should not be called chromatic *adaptation*. The word adaptation rather implies that it was evolved because it was useful to the plant, and therefore was preserved and augmented by the action of natural selection. This is fine, but we must remember that the pigments of the seaweeds may have appeared for some totally different reason, quite unconnected with photosynthesis, and been made use of later to assist photosynthesis in those seaweeds that possessed them.

It is very unlikely that we shall ever know the answer.

Other brown seaweeds

The fucales and the Laminariales include most of the British seaweeds that are familiar on account of their large size and the abundance with which they occur on rocky shores. There are, however, many other species of brown seaweeds which are nearly, if not quite, as common. Some are small, even microscopic, but others are of quite a fair size.

THE SEA SORREL

Sea sorrel (Oseille de mer) is the name given by the people of the French coast to species of *Desmarestia*, brown seaweeds growing in deep water. They are called sea sorrel because when they start to decompose, which they do with great rapidity after being collected, they change colour to a bright bluish-green, like verdigris. If sea sorrels are collected with other seaweeds they should be placed in a separate container; otherwise, the rot will quickly spread to the rest of the collection. The rot seems to be due to the liberation of acid from the plants; the nature of the acid is still a matter of argument among phycologists, but it is thought to be principally sulphuric acid.

Species of *Desmarestia* are mainly confined to the cooler seas. They reach their largest size in the Pacific Ocean, but Atlantic species can attain a length of two to three feet. They normally grow in several fathoms of water, so that they are not uncovered by the tide, but specimens are frequently washed up on the beach after storms, and they are also often found entangled with floating fragments of other seaweeds.

The erect frond of *Desmarestia* arises from a disk-shaped holdfast. The frond is flattened, and regularly branched on either side of the main rachis. The branches bear secondary branches, which themselves may bear tertiary branches in the form of filaments (Fig. 30). The filaments of perennial species are deciduous, falling off during the winter. The denuded appearance of the winter plants may trap the unwary into thinking that they are of a different genus (lower part of Fig. 30).

FIGURE 30.
Desmarestia aculeata

The sporangia are borne on slightly raised portions of the frond. The zoöspores, when liberated, give rise to minute gametophytic plants. The male gametophyte, which is smaller than the female, produce antheridia each of which forms a single sperm; the larger female plants produce swollen oögonia, each of which forms one egg cell. The fertilized egg cell grows into a

FIGURE 31.
Part of a frond of Desmarestia viridis.

new *Desmarestia* plant. The alternation of generations is therefore heteromorphic, as in the Laminariales.

Four species of *Desmarestia* are found round the coasts of
Britain. *D. aculeata* is a perennial about three feet long (Fig.30).
Tangled masses of old plants washed ashore by the waves are
sometimes known as "landlady's wig". Specimens of *D.
aculeata* are sometimes found entangled with the stipes of the
cuvie. *D. viridis* is smaller than *D. aculeata*, and can be distinguished from it by the fact that the branches are opposite
to one another, whereas in *D. aculeata* they are alternate (Fig.
31). *D. ligulata* is about the same size as *D. aculeata* but is
easily distinguished from it by its flattened frond, which has a
leafy appearance owing to its lance-shaped branches (Fig. 32).
Young specimens of *D. ligulata* are particularly attractive to
mount, as they stick to the paper without the use of adhesive.

Desmarestia dudresnayi, the fourth British species of *Desmarestia*, is a rare plant, It has opposite branches, and in British
waters it is confined to southern England and Ireland.

Arthrocladia, the other British member of the family Desmares-
tiaceae, also occurs in deep water, growing on rocks, shells, and
sometimes on the marine flowering plant *Zostera*, or eel-grass.
It can be distinguished from *Desmarestia* by its widely spreading,
opposite branches and slender habit. The third member of the
small family, *Phaeurus*, occurs only in the Antarctic.

THE SCYTOSIPHONACEAE
The Scytosiphonaceae is a family which contains seaweeds
which, at first sight, would appear to be of very different
structure and habit; the beginner would not dream of placing
all the various genera in the same family. They are, however,

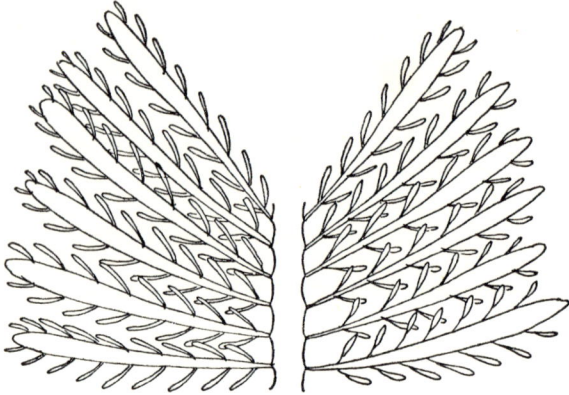

FIGURE 32.
Part of a frond of Desmarestia ligulata.

all similar in certain minutiæ of internal structure and life history. As far as we are concerned, the main thing is the appearance in the Scytosiphonaceae of a sporangium of a type that we have not met before.

The sporangia of all the brown seaweeds we have so far dealt with agree in one thing: they are uniloculor. This means that they consist of one cell, and that they are not subdivided by cross-walls (septa) into a number of different compartments.

In the Scytosiphonaceae the sporangia are plurilocular: that is, they are divided by transverse cross-walls, and sometimes by longitudinal ones as well, into a number of separate compartments, each of which produces a single zoöspore. Some seaweeds have both unilocular and plurilocular sporangia, but the Scytosiphonaceae, as far as is at present known (the life histories of some members of the family have not been completely worked out), have plurilocular sporangia only. There appears to be no alternation of generations, though again we must await a complete knowledge of the life histories of all members of the family before we can be quite certain.

The commonest British member of the Scytosiphonaceae is *Scytosiphon lomentaria*, which is an extremely common seaweed on rocky shores all round Britain; it is also widely distributed throughout the temperate regions of the world in both hemispheres. It grows in tufts on rocks and on stones in rock pools in

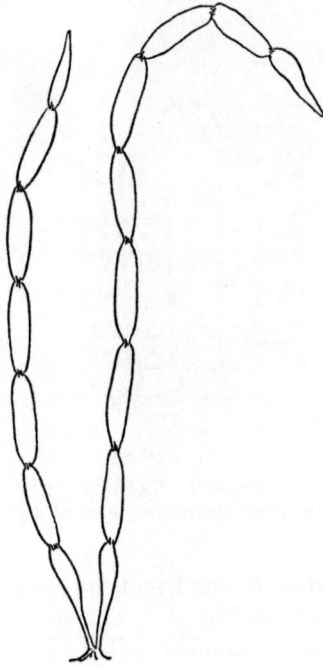

FIGURE 33.
Scytosiphon lomentaria.

the intertidal zone; sometimes it is found growing as an epiphyte, perched on another seaweed.

S. lomentaria is a great migrant, for as the temperature rises with the advance of summer, fresh generations move down towards the sea.

S. lomentaria, like all other members of the Scytosiphonaceae, is most plentiful in the winter.

Plants of *S. lomentaria* consist of a minute holdfast, from which arise the fronds. At first the plants are like solid hairs sticking up from the holdfast, but as they grow they increase in diameter until they are up to a quarter of an inch wide, and hollow. The mature fronds are from six to eighteen inches long, with pointed or rounded tips, and the fronds are cut into a number of lobes by constrictions about one to one and a half inches apart (Fig. 33).

The plurilocular sporangia of *Scytosiphon lomentaria* are

3*

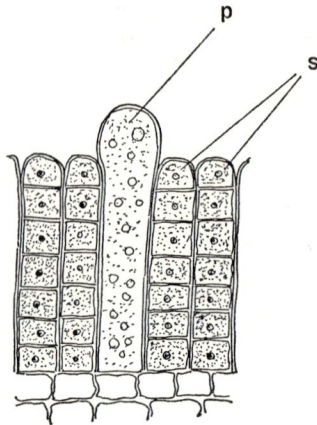

FIGURE 34.
Section through part of the fertile region of Scytosiphon lomentaria,
showing plurilocular sporangia (s) and a paraphysis (p).

formed on the surface of the frond, interspersed with ovoid or pear-shaped paraphyses (Fig. 34). The zoöspores germinate and grow into a microscopic filament called a protonema, from which a branch develops into a new *Scytosiphon* plant. There is no alternation of generations.

THE OYSTER THIEF

This amusing little seaweed was named oyster thief ((''voleuse d'huitres'') by the French oyster growers at Vannes. Its scientific name is *Colpomenia peregrina*. The frond is spherical and hollow like a balloon; it is from half an inch to (exceptionally) nine inches in diameter (Fig. 35). The seaweed is usually an epiphyte, attaching itself to the fronds of other seaweeds by means of its small holdfast. During the early part of the present century it appeared on the Atlantic coast of France, as well as on our own south coast, and it frequently used to attach itself to oysters, lifting them from the oyster beds by the buoyancy of its balloon-like fronds and carrying them away with the tide— hence the name oyster thief.

Fortunately for the oyster growers, the oyster thief cannot compete with other seaweeds, such as *Enteromorpha*, which

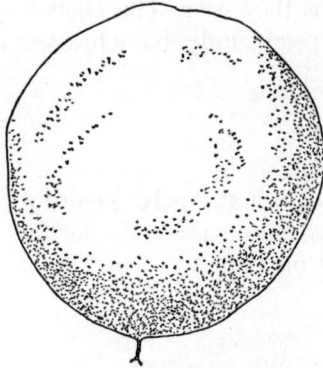

FIGURE 35.
The oyster thief (Colpomenia peregrina).

grow more strongly. It is no longer a serious pest in the oyster beds.

The bladders of the oyster thief are greenish when young, but as the plant grows older they become olive-brown. When mature they become covered with small brown specks which mark the position of the plurilocular sporangia. The life history of the oyster thief appears to be similar to that of *Scytosiphon*, though there are points that have not yet been thoroughly investigated.

THE DICTYOTACEAE

The Dictyotaceae show certain characteristics that mark them off distinctly from other brown seaweeds. Chief of these is that their asexual spores are not motile. On account of this unique feature they were at one time thought to be a group quite distinct from the rest of the brown seaweeds, or Phaeophyta. This is now known not to be the case, as the Dictyotaceae have many other features that they share with the other brown seaweeds. In particular, their antheridia are similar to the antheridia found in the rest of the Phaeophyta.

The Dictyotaceae are quite a small family, all with thin fronds which may be strap-like or fan-shaped. There is an isomorphic alternation of generations: the sporophytic plants resemble the gametophytes exactly except in the kind of reproductive organs they bear. The Dictyotaceae are a mainly tropical and subtropical family, but a few species grow in cooler waters.

DICTYOTA DICHOTOMA

Dictyota dichotoma is extremely plentiful in the south of England, but it becomes scarcer the farther north we travel. It is also common on both the Atlantic and Pacific coasts of America.

FIGURE 36.
Dictyota dichotoma.

Dictyota dichotoma is a delicate, translucent seaweed, from four to six inches long. The frond is ribbon-like, about one-fifth of an inch wide, and branched in a regularly dichotomous manner (Fig. 36); it is only three cells thick, a layer of large, cubical cells being sandwiched between two layers of smaller cells (Fig. 37a). Their thinness makes the fronds rather limp, so that they are difficult to spread out evenly on blotting paper when drying specimens for the seaweed collection. Its colour varies from orange-green to yellowish-brown, and if the upper part of the frond is examined carefully a number of minute dark brown spots can be seen; these mark the position of the reproductive organs.

Dictyota dichotoma grows in the sublittoral zone, just below low-tide mark, but it can frequently be found growing in rock pools low down on the beach. It often shows a beautiful iridescent colouring when seen growing below the water.

The growth of *Dictyota dichotoma* takes place at the tips of the branches of the frond, where there is a special kind of cell known as the apical cell (Fig. 37b). This cell is lens-shaped, and is continually dividing, cutting off new cells along its backward face. When the frond branches, the apical cell divides vertically, the two daughter cells so formed going their own way and giving rise to a branch.

A remarkable feature of *Dictyota dichotoma* is the way in which it is tied to the periodicity of the tides in the liberation of its gametes (sex cells). When *D. dichotoma* is growing in European waters it liberates its gametes once a fortnight. On the coasts of England the sex organs begin to develop during one spring tide and the gametes are set free a fortnight later,

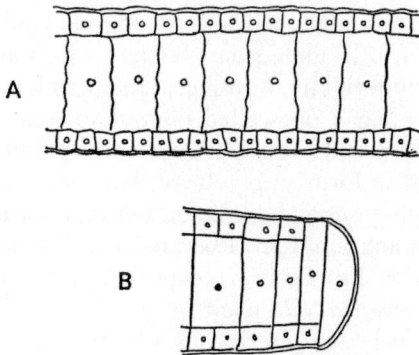

FIGURE 37.
Dictyota dichotoma. *A, Section of part of the frond. B, Section through growing point, showing the apical cell. Greatly magnified.*

during the next spring tide. In the Mediterranean it behaves differently. At Naples, the sex organs begin to develop during a neap tide, and the gametes are set free on the next neap tide. On the Atlantic coast of North Carolina the gametes are only liberated once per lunar month; what is more, they are always set free on the spring tides of the full moon, whether they happen to be the greater series of spring tides or the lesser.

From this, it is clear that the life history of *Dictyota dichotoma* is linked in some way with the cycle of the tides, but the way in which this linkage works is not at all clear. The fortnightly period of *D. dichotoma* is maintained even when the plants are removed from the sea and grown in a tank in the laboratory.

The sex organs are produced on both sides of the frond, occurring in groups or sori; the antheridia and oögonia are formed on different plants. The oögonial sori can be distinguished from the antheridial sori by their deeper colour. Each antheridium in a male sorus is formed from a cell belonging to the outer layer of the frond, which divides transversely, forming a lower stalk cell and an upper antheridial initial; the latter then divides several times, forming a multicellular antheridium each cell of which forms a single sperm. As the antheridia complete their development the cells surrounding the sorus grow out to form a frill, or involucre, round the sorus (Plate 10 and Fig. 38).

The development of the oögonia in a female sorus is similar to that of the antheridia, a cell of the outer layer of the frond dividing to form a stalk cell and an oögonial initial. Whereas the antheridial cell undergoes further divisions to form a multicellular antheridium, however, the oögonial initial remains undivided, forming a one-celled oögonium containing a single egg cell (Plate 11 and Fig. 39). Cells surrounding the oögonial sorus grow out to form an involucre, but this is not so large as the involucre that surrounds the antheridial sorus.

The sperms and eggs are liberated into the sea water, and after fertilization has been accomplished a fertilized egg cell grows into a new *Dictyota* plant.

The plant that I have described is, of course, the gametophyte, since it bore the sex organs. The new plant is the sporophyte. This resembles the gametophyte in all particulars except its reproductive organs, which are sporangia producing spores. The sporangia, like the sex organs, are formed in sori on either side

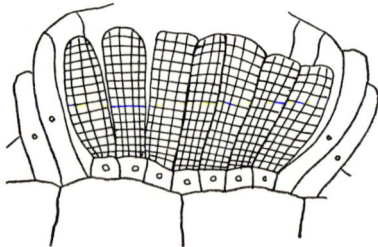

FIGURE 38.
Dictyota dichotoma; *section through an antheridial sorus, greatly magnified.*

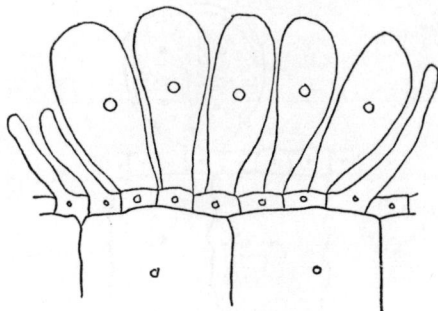

FIGURE 39.
Dictyota dichotoma; *section through an oögonial sorus, greatly
magnified.*

of the frond. The early development of a sporangium is similar
to that of an antheridium or oögonium. A cell of the outer layer
of the frond grows out to about twice its normal height, and
divides transversely to form a stalk cell and a sporangial initial.
The sporangial initial cell then grows enormously, becoming
spherical and about twice the diameter of the thallus. Its nucleus
divides twice, and four spores are formed in each sporangium;
these are called tetraspores because of their number (Fig. 40).

When the tetraspores germinate they grow into gametophytic plants, and the life cycle is repeated. *Dictyota* is the first
example we have had of a seaweed with an isomorphic alternation of generations; there is nothing whatsoever to distinguish the gametophytic plants from the sporophytes except the
fact that the former bear sex organs while the latter bear
sporangia. The gametophyte generation is haploid and the
sporophyte diploid, meiosis taking place when the nucleus of
the tetrasporangium divides twice to form the four tetraspores.

The sex of the gametophyte is determined when the tetraspores are formed, for two of the four tetraspores always develop
into male gametophytes while the other two form female
gametophytes.

THE PEACOCK'S TAIL
The peacock's tail, *Padina pavonia*, is another member of the
Dictyotaceae that is to be found on beaches in the south of

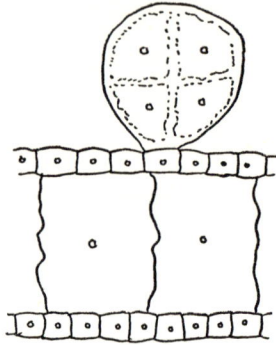

FIGURE 40.
Dictyota dichotoma; *developing tetrasporangium, greatly magnified.*

England between about midsummer and the approach of winter. The genus *Padina* is tropical or subtropical, and the peacock's tail is the only species that can live as far north as Britain. It occurs in sunny positions in rock pools situated between the tide marks, often growing on the sunny side of rocky ledges.

The name peacock's tail suggests a seaweed dressed in many bright colours, but here I must disappoint you, for the peacock's tail is really a rather-dull-looking seaweed, though exceedingly beautiful in its form. It grows from a small holdfast, which gives rise to a short stipe; this in turn expands to form a fan-shaped frond of extremely graceful appearance. The frond is usually from two to four inches wide, thin and concave with a somewhat frilled margin. The upper surface of the frond is often covered with a white coating of lime, while the lower surface is coloured with bands of light brown, dark brown, and olive-green (Fig. 41).

The peacock's tail has a similar life history to that of *Dictyota*, but the alternation of generations is less regular. Sporophyte and gametophyte resemble one another closely, the reproductive organs being borne on the surface of the frond. Frequently the entire contents of the tetrasporangium germinate and grow into a new sporophyte, missing out the gametophyte; in such cases, tetraspores are not formed, and meiosis does not take place. In some districts only the sporophytic plants are found, the gametophyte generation having apparently disappeared altogether.

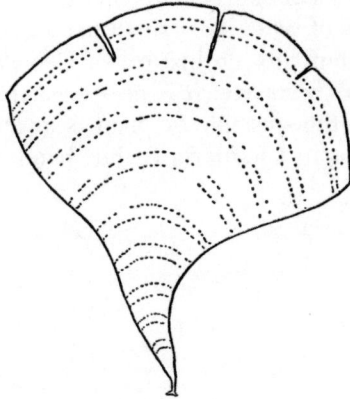

FIGURE 41.
The peacock's tail (Padina pavonia).

THE CHORDARIACEAE

The Chordariaceae is a family of seaweeds in which the frond is cylindrical and branching. The cells that make up the rather loosely-connected tissue are embedded in a jelly-like material, making the plants slimy to the touch.

The commonest member of the family round British shores is *Chordaria flagelliformis*, an annual seaweed that grows, attached to stones or rocks, in the littoral zone. A small holdfast produces a frond which consists of a slender, cylindrical central axis giving off similar lateral branches (Fig. 42). The frond is somewhat brittle, and extremely slimy to the touch. The plants are normally from six inches to two feet long. The name *flagelliformis* comes from the Latin word *flagellum*, meaning a whip, and this is the general impression given by the plant. The central axis of the frond gives off many longish lateral branches which are themselves whip-like. The colour of the frond is dark brown.

The frond of *C. flagelliformis* is covered with microscopic hairs, the cells of which contain abundant chloroplasts. Most of the work of photosynthesis is performed by these hairs. The unilocular sporangia are scattered among the hairs; they produce zoöspores which germinate to form microscopic gametophytic plants, which in turn produce plurilocular sporangia in which the gametes are formed. The gametes are microscopic, flagellated cells resembling the zoöspores. It is believed that there are gametes of two kinds: small male gametes and larger female gametes, but the life history of Chordaria has not yet been followed with certainty. It is presumed that after fusion of a pair of gametes the sporophytic plant is formed. The alternation of generations in Chordaria is thus heteromorphic.

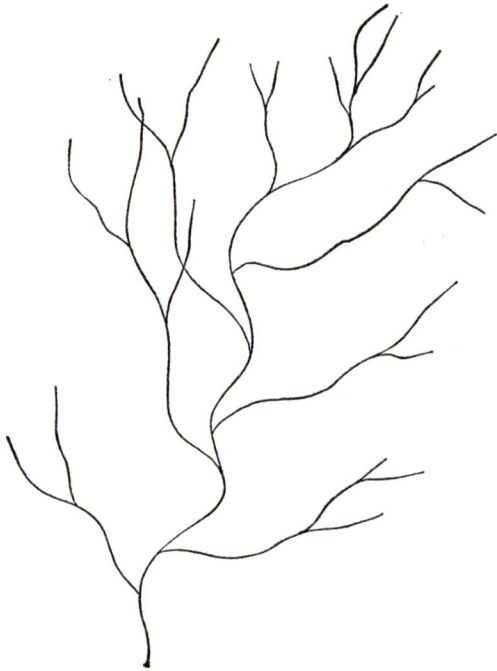

FIGURE 42.
Chordaria flagelliformis.

THE CORYNOPHLOEACEAE

The Corynophloeaceae is related to the Chordariaceae, both families belonging to the order Chordariales. Like the Chordariaceae, the Corynophloeaceae have a heteromorphic alternation of generations.

Leathesia difformis is a common British member of the Corynophloeaceae, growing on rocks between the tide marks, or as an epiphyte on other seaweeds. The frond of *Leathesia* is in the form of a rounded cushion, hollow at the centre, and with a diameter of from half an inch to two inches. The inside of the cushion is formed from radiating, branched filaments of cells closely packed together; towards the outside of the cushion these bear small, densely packed filaments containing chloroplasts and responsible for photosynthesis.

The frond of *Leathesia difformis* is not unlike that of the oyster thief, especially when dried. It can be distinguished from the oyster thief when in the water by its thick-walled, shiny fronds, whereas the fronds of the oyster thief are dull and thin-walled. The fronds of *Leathesia* become more or less lobed when mature (Fig. 43), while those of the oyster thief are always spherical, without lobes or folds.

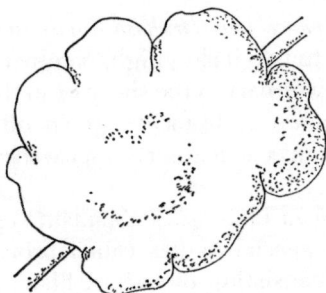

FIGURE 43.
Leathesia difformis.

The fronds of *Leathesia* bear both unilocular and plurilocular sporangia, which are formed near the bases of the photosynthetic filaments. The unilocular sporangia are formed first, and the zoöspores from them germinate to form small, disk-like plants bearing plurilocular sporangia which produce gametes. Fusion of gametes gives rise to the normal-sized plants, which are the sporophytes. The alternation of generations is thus heteromorphic.

Besides the unilocular sporangia, the sporophytic (normal-sized) plant may produce plurilocular sporangia. These are usually formed later than the unilocular sporangia, and in appearance they resemble those of the gametophyte. Instead of producing gametes, however, the plurilocular sporangia on the sporophytic plants produce zoöspores which germinate to

reproduce the sporophyte directly. This can be regarded as an
accessory means of reproduction.

THE SPHACELARIACEAE
The Sphacelariaceae are small seaweeds belonging to an order,
the Sphacelariales, which is mainly represented in the Southern
Hemisphere. Some of the Sphacelariaceae, however, are British
and among these, *Spacelaria cirrhosa* is a common epiphyte,
growing on a great variety of other seaweeds, green, brown,
and red.

SPHACELARIA CIRRHOSA
The fronds of *Sphacelaria cirrhosa* form dense tufts, from a
quarter of an inch to two inches high, on other seaweeds, usually
growing on the lower part of the shore or in the sublittoral zone.
Owing to the numerous branches given off from the central
axis (Fig. 44), it has a feathery appearance when examined
with a hand lens.

Sphacelaria cirrhosa undergoes abundant vegetative reproduction by means of special bodies called propagules. These are
minute branches, consisting of a short filament of cells, usually

FIGURE 44.
Sphacelaria cirrhosa.

with three short branches at one end. The propagules become detached from the parent plant and grow into new plants resembling the one from which they originated. *S. cirrhosa* seems to rely mainly on its propagules for reproduction.

The life history of *Sphacelaria cirrhosa* has not been followed completely, but more is known about the life history of the related species, *S. bipinnata*, which probably resembles that of *S. cirrhosa* in its general details. The sporophytic plants of both species bear both unilocular and plurilocular sporangia. In *S. bipinnata* the unilocular sporangia produce haploid gametes, meiosis occurring in the sporangia. These gametes come together in clumps, where fusion between pairs of gametes is presumed to occur, and from the fused gametes the gametophytes are produced. The gametophytes resemble the sporophytes, alternation of generations being isomorphic; they bear plurilocular sporangia, the spores from which reproduce the sporophyte again.

The plurilocular sporangia borne by the sporophyte produce zoöspores which reproduce the sporophyte again directly the gametophyte generation being in this case missed out. These spores can be regarded as an accessory means of reproduction.

Another member of the Sphacelariaceae is *Halopteris*, a genus of small to medium-sized seaweeds characteristic of warmer

FIGURE 45.
Halopteris scoparia.

waters, but with a few species that are found on British coasts, especially towards the south. *Halopteris scoparia* is a tufted plant, from two to six inches in height, with the holdfast and the lower part of the stipe covered with brown fibres, giving the plant a somewhat shaggy appearance. The frond of *H. scoparia* is alternately branched, the branches bearing short secondary branches, alternating regularly (Fig. 45). The bushy appearance disappears in the winter, so that winter plants could be mistaken for a different species of seaweed.

Halopteris scoparia is quite common in tidal pools low down on the shore, and in the sea below low-tide mark. It often grows on rocks which are covered with sand.

THE ECTOCARPACEAE

The Ectocarpaceae contain some of the smallest of the brown seaweeds, including many species that are epiphytes on larger seaweeds. A few species are mildly parasitic. The life histories of some members of the Ectocarpaceae, and particularly of some species of *Ectocarpus*, present certain interesting points to the botanist, and we are awaiting the results of further research to elucidate some of the facts. To the collector the Ectocarpaceae may be a little dull on account of their small size, but some of them are extremely common, and no account of the brown seaweeds could miss them out.

FIGURE 46.
Ectocarpus confervoides.

ECTOCARPUS

The frond of *Ectocarpus* consists of a branching filament of cells; in some species the filament is microscopic, while in others it may reach a length of several inches. The filaments are of two kinds: there is a prostrate filament which runs along the substratum, and this gives off a series of vertical filaments. This is known as a heterotrichous filament.

As an example of the genus *Ectocarpus* I am going to describe *E. confervoides*, the commonest British species; it is also the largest species found on British coasts. The life history of *E. confervoides* is typical of the genus, and, with minor modifications, will fit almost any species.

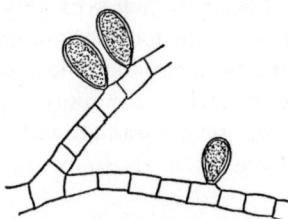

FIGURE 47.
Ectocarpus: *unilocular sporangia, greatly magnified.*

Ectocarpus confervoides grows on rocks, and as an epiphyte on the larger brown seaweeds, from the middle of the littoral zone down into the sublittoral zone. It is plentiful in almost any coastal area of Britain (Fig. 46). The filaments are often twisted round one another to give the appearance of a piece of string; the only seaweed that the beginner is likely to confuse it with is *E. tomentosus*. To separate these two species a microscope is needed, but the twisting of the filaments is much more pronounced in *E. tomentosus* than in *E. confervoides*. The colour of the frond is yellowish brown or olive-green.

Ectocarpus confervoides has an isomorphic alternation of generations. The sporophyte bears both unilocular and plurilocular sporangia. The zoöspores from the unilocular sporangia (Plate 12 and Fig. 47) are haploid, meiosis having taken place in the sporangium during their formation, while the zoöspores from the plurilocular sporangia (Plate 13 and Fig. 48) are diploid, like the parent plant. The zoöspores from the plurilocular sporangia reproduce the sporophyte again: they are an

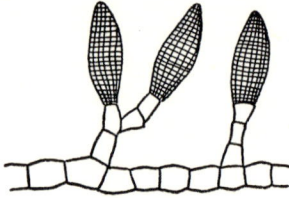

FIGURE 48.
Ectocarpus: *plurilocular sporangia, greatly magnified.*

accessory method of reproduction. The haploid zoöspores from the unilocular sporangia, on the other hand, produce the gametophyte generation. These are plants exactly like the sporophyte, except that they produce plurilocular sporangia only; the spores from these, on germination, produce the sporophyte generation.

The gametophyte, as well as the sporophyte, has its accessory means of reproduction, for if a gamete fails to pair with another gamete it may behave as a zoöspore and grow into a new *gametophyte*.

Ectocarpus does not always stick strictly to its regular life cycle. The life histories of all the species have not yet been elucidated, but some interesting facts are known about the behaviour of *E. siliculosus*. Plants of this species from British and Swedish waters appear to be all sporophytic, the gametophyte never appearing. In the Bay of Naples, on the other hand, the plants are nearly all gametophytes, the sporophyte being seldom found. The difference in behaviour of the same seaweed in the two localities probably depends on the difference in temperature, or possibly on the strong sunlight and clear water in the Mediterranean compared with the conditions in Britain and Sweden. At Woods Hole, in Massachusetts, both sporophyte and gametophyte generations occur with equal abundance.

****
* 5 *
****

The red seaweeds

To the layman, the red seaweeds, or Rhodophyta, are less familiar than the brown seaweeds, though they are in fact common enough. For one thing, the red seaweeds are smaller than the large brown seaweeds such as species of *Fucus* and *Laminaria*. For another, they are, in the main, deep-water seaweeds, growing below the low-tide mark, or in deep rock pools, where they are never uncovered by the tide. If you climb along the rocks of a Cornish cove at low tide you will find plenty of red seaweeds attached to the rocks below the water. Do not expect them all to be red, however, for a "red" seaweed can be any colour you like to name.

The chromatophores of the red seaweeds contain, besides the usual chlorophylls, xanthophylls, and carotenes, two other accessory pigments: phycoerythrin, which is red, and phycocyanin, which is blue. The two latter pigments are of the class known as phycobilins; their proportions in the chromatophores vary greatly between different species, so that the colour of the seaweed can be anything from red to blue.

The cells of most red seaweeds have cell walls of two layers the outer one being composed of pectic compounds and the inner one of cellulose. The pectic compounds in the outer layer may give rise to water-soluble pectin, which forms a slimy covering to the seaweed. In most of the higher red algae (Florideae) the cells are connected with one another by wide openings in the cell walls; these openings are traversed by protoplasmic strands.

Many of the Florideae are iridescent, the effect being produced by yellowish bodies, apparently composed of protein, in their cells. These reflect light of short wavelength. When the seaweed is growing in strong light the yellow bodies arrange

themselves along the outer walls of the cells, while the chloroplasts take up positions along the side walls; if the illumination
is faint these positions are reversed.

The structure of the frond in the red seaweeds is basically
filamentous, but nonetheless it reaches a high degree of complexity in many species. There are two general plans on which
the frond may be built up. In the uniaxial type there is one main
filament bearing the branches of which the bulk of the frond is
composed. This filament may consist of a single strand of cells,
but frequently it is corticated: i.e. it has a number of cells surrounding the central filament. In the multiaxial type of frond,
also known as the fountain type, there is a mass of central filaments forming a sort of cable, with branches spraying out
towards the surface. The central filaments usually form a solid
core, but they may be arranged in a ring round a central cavity.
The central strand and its branches are often embedded in a
gelatinous substance which hides the filamentous nature of the
frond, giving the impression of a solid mass of tissue.

The life histories of the more advanced red seaweeds are
extremely complex, often involving an alternation of three
generations instead of the more usual two.

The red algae are predominantly marine, though a few are
found in fresh water. A few of the simpler species consist of a
single microscopic cell. The phylum Rhodophyta contains but
a single class, the Rhodophyceae, which is divided into two very
unequal sub-classes, the Bangioideae and the Florideae. Of
these, the Bangioideae is the smaller and the more primitive
group, simpler both in the construction of their fronds and in
their life histories.

THE BANGIOIDEAE

The Bangioideae are sometimes known as the Protoflorideae.
The plants are all simple in structure. A few are unicellular,
while the remainder consist of a branched uniaxial filament,
which may have the filament and its branches enclosed in gelatinous material so that the frond appears to be membraneous.

The cells of the Bangioideae each contain a single large
chromatophore, which is placed near the centre of the cell. The
life history does not show the extreme complications that are

found in the Florideae. A few genera, such as *Porphyridum*, are unicellular, the cells being stuck together by gelatinous material to form colonies; *Porphyridum* occurs in the soil. Other soil and fresh-water forms, such as *Asterocystis*, have their single cells stuck together end to end by mucilage, so that they have the appearance of being filamentous. The majority of Bangioideae, however, are marine plants of simple construction.

THE PURPLE LAVER

The purple laver, *Porphyra umbilicalis*, is well known as an edible seaweed; it is rich in protein, and also is a good source of vitamins B and C.

The frond of the purple laver grows from a disk-shaped holdfast, and is variable in shape; it may be anything from strap-shaped to semi-circular (Fig. 49). When the plants are strap-shaped the frond may be up to two feet long and three or four inches wide. The colour is also extremely variable. Typically, the purple laver is a beautiful rosy purple, but it may be pale purple, reddish, olive-green, or even brown.

FIGURE 49.
The purple laver (Porphyra umbilicalis).

The purple laver is an extremely adaptable seaweed, for it grows well under a variety of different conditions. On rocky shores it forms dense colonies on rocks and stones, and, in spite of the extreme delicacy of the frond, which is only one or two cells thick, it does not appear to be harmed in any way if it is left uncovered by the tide for a spell. Should this happen, the fronds lie flat against the rocks until the returning tide covers them again, when the plants resume their normal appearance. To see it at its best in this country one should look for it in the winter, though in northern regions it remains well developed throughout the year.

The one or two layers of cells that compose the frond of the purple laver are embedded in a tough matrix of gelatinous material. In the purple laver, and in most other species of *Porphyra*, the cells each contain a single chromatophore, which is more or less star-shaped and placed in the middle of the cell; a few species of *Porphyra* have two chromatophores per cell. As the frond grows by cell division the divisions are always in a plane perpendicular to the surface, so that the frond increases in area without any increase in thickness.

The male reproductive cells of the purple laver are called spermatia, and, like the male gametes of all red seaweeds, they have no flagella or other means of locomotion, depending on currents in the water to carry them to the female cells. They are formed in organs called spermogonia which in *Porphyra* are simply cells of the frond; these divide, both vertically and transversely, forming 16, 32, 64, or 128 spermatia. When the receding tide exposes the frond the gelatinous matrix shrinks a little, so that the spermatia are squeezed out of the frond, much as toothpaste is squeezed out of a tube.

The female sex organs are called carpogonia and, like the spermogonia, they are only slightly modified vegetative cells. They increase in length, and an outgrowth develops at one end which may or may not reach the surface of the gelatinous material in which the frond is embedded. This elongation functions as a trichogyne—the name given in the red seaweeds to an extension of the carpogonium on which the spermatia settle. If these outgrowths reach the surface of the frond the spermatia, brought by currents in the water, adhere to them. If the trichogynes are not long enough for this the spermatia settle on the surface of the frond and put out protoplasmic "feelers" which connect with the trichogynes. A nucleus from a spermatium then passes along the protoplasmic process into a trichogyne, and down it into the carpogonium, where it fuses with the egg cell in the carpogonium and fertilizes it.

When fertilized, the egg cell immediately divides, forming from two to thirty-two spores which are called carpospores. Like the spermatia, the carpospores are discharged when the frond is washed by the incoming tide. The carpospores germinate to produce small filaments that bore into the shells of marine molluscs, and it has recently been shown that these filaments are identical with a small red seaweed that was formerly known as *Conchocelis rosea*.

What happens next is still a matter of dispute among phycologists. The *Conchocelis* produces spores known as conchospores. These have not yet been seen to germinate, so we do not know whether they reproduce the *Porphyra* stage of the life history, or whether they produce more of the *Conchocelis*. More work is needed on the life history of *Porphyra*.

Porphyra also produces monospores, so called because only one is formed from each monosporangium. These are an asexual form of reproduction, and they reproduce the *Porphyra* form directly.

The purple laver is used in Britain for making laver bread, the plants being boiled to produce a jelly which can then be covered with oatmeal and fried. In Ireland it is called "sloke" and is sometimes seen in fishmongers' shops. The main centre of *Porphyra* eating, however, is Japan, where *P. tenera*, a species closely related to the purple laver, is cultivated on seaweed "farms", a practice that has been going on for at least 300 years. The Japanese farmers sink bundles of bamboo shoots in the mud at a depth of about six feet. Monospores are produced in large numbers by *P. tenera*, one square centimetre of the frond yielding about 10,000 of them. The monospores settle on the bamboo shoots and germinate; when the shoots are well covered with young plants they are taken to an estuary, where the young seaweeds grow to maturity. When the fronds are finally harvested they are washed, chopped, and set out on trays to dry. *Porphyra* is particularly in demand as a covering to balls of rice, which the Japanese use in much the same way as bread rolls are used in this country.

P. leucosticta is a species that is quite common during spring and early summer, growing on rocks and stones, and sometimes as an epiphyte on other seaweeds. It closely resembles *P. umbilicalis*, but can be distinguished from it by the fact that the spermatia are formed in longitudinal patches on the surface of the frond, whereas in *P. umbilicalis* they occur along the edges. The position of the spermatia is readily seen by the discoloration of the frond, which becomes yellowish-white where they are developing.

BANGIA

Bangia is a seaweed with gelatinous fronds which are thread-like and unbranched. The commonest species is *Bangia fusco-purpurea*, which is found covering rocks and woodwork with what looks like a dense fleece. It is not uncommon. The filaments are blackish-purple, and usually from two to six inches long. It reproduces by means of spermatia and carpogonia in much the same way as the purple laver.

THE FLORIDEAE

The bulk of the red seaweeds belong to the Florideae, and, as I have already said, their life histories can be extremely complex. They are all basically filamentous in structure, but their filamentous nature is often hidden by the fact that the filaments are bound together by gelatinous material.

Growth in the Florideae is always apical, a single apical cell at the end of the filament dividing to form new cells behind it. Each branch also has its own growing apical cell at its tip, and in the multiaxial or fountain type of frond (see page 90) each filament making up the central strand also has its own apical cell, by the activity of which it grows. In a multiaxial frond no particular apical cell dominates the rest, so that each of the filaments grows at approximately the same rate. When a lateral branch develops on a multiaxial filament it always forms on the outside of the central strand, so that the frond, when mature, has a central portion, consisting of the main filament running lengthways, with a surrounding layer of lateral branches.

The structure of the frond in the Florideae is made more complex by the cells not necessarily being of the same size. We commonly find a central region, or medulla, formed of large cells, surrounded by a cortex of smaller cells.

Reproduction in the Florideae is extremely complex, and in many cases the sexual process has not been followed out completely, so that certain stages are either unknown or only a matter of guesswork. There is a great deal of variation between the reproductive processes in the different groups of the Florideae.

The male sex organ, or antheridium, is developed from an antheridial mother cell, which is usually carried on a special filament. In the more advanced Florideae the antheridial mother cell forms an outgrowth from which the antheridium develops, its contents forming a single spermatium. The spermatia of the red seaweeds are always non-motile, relying on currents in the water to reach the carpogonia, or female reproductive organs. When an antheridium has liberated its single spermatium it may form another.

The female sex organs, which are called carpogonia, are formed on special carpogonial filaments, which are carried on lateral branches of the ordinary vegetative filaments. The cells which subtend carpogonial filaments are quite short, and they can usually be recognized under the microscope by the fact that they are without chloroplasts. At the end of each carpogonium is a prolongation, not unlike the trunk of an elephant, called the trichogyne. The trichogyne may be short or long.

When the spermatia from the antheridia are set free currents in the water carry some of them to the trichogyne of a carpogonium, where they stick. The nuclei of the spermatia enter the trichogyne of the carpogonium and pass down it into the carpogonium itself, where one of them fuses with the carpogonial nucleus.

The fusion of a male nucleus from a spermatium with the female nucleus in the carpogonium constitutes the main act of fertilization, but it is by no means the end of the reproductive process. After the sexual fusion, all kinds of complications begin. The nature of these complications depends upon what group of the Florideae the particular seaweed belong to.

In the simpler members of the Florideae short filaments,

called gonimoblast filaments, grow out from the fertilized carpogonium. On the ends of the gonimoblast filaments sporangia called carposporangia, are formed. The carposporangia contain carpospores which, when liberated, germinate to produce another plant bearing antheridia and carpogonia. The Nemalioales have a relatively simple life history of this kind.

The main plant which bears the antheridia and carpogonia is clearly the gametophyte generation, since it produces the gametes. The gonimoblast filaments grow from the fertilized carpogonia and produce carposporangia at their tips; they therefore constitute the sporophyte generation, which in this case is parasitic on the gametophyte. It is usually known as the carposporophyte, to distinguish it from *another* sporophyte generation, the tetrasporophyte, which appears in the life histories of some of the more advanced Florideae.

According to the degree of complexity in their reproductive processes the Florideae can be divided into six orders. These are the Nemalionales, the Gelidiales, the Cryptonemiales, the Gigartinales, the Rhodymeniales, and the Ceramiales. The orders are further subdivided into families.

THE NEMALIONALES

This is the simplest order in the Florideae. *Nemalion elmin-*

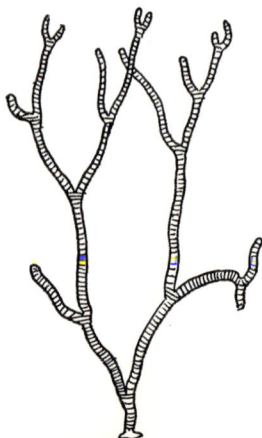

FIGURE 50.
Nemalion elminthoides.

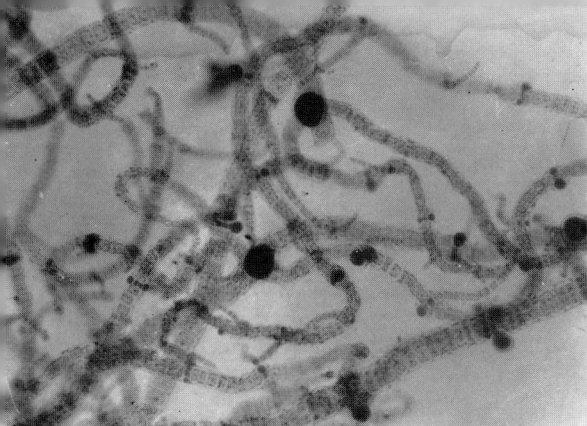

Plate 12. Photomicrograph of *Ectocarpus*, showing unilocular sporangia.

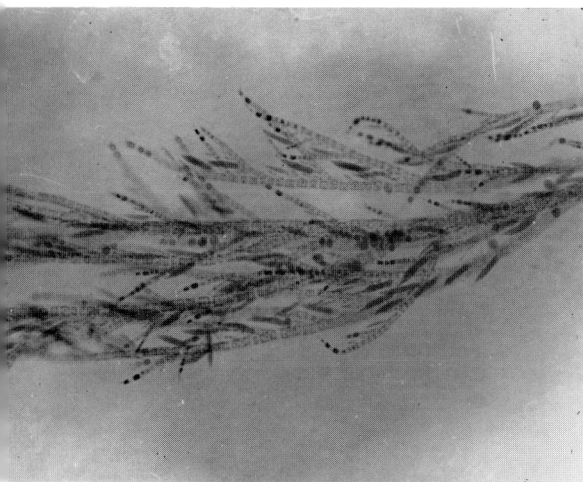

Plate 13. Photomicrograph of *Ectocarpus*, showing plurilocular sporangia.

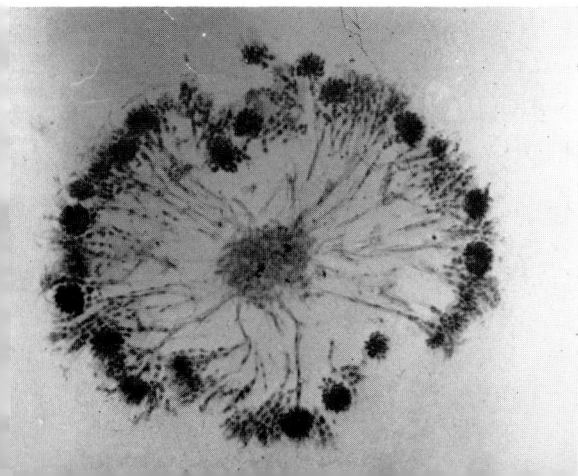

Plate 14. Photomicrograph of a transverse section of the frond of *Nemalion*, showing its filamentous structure.

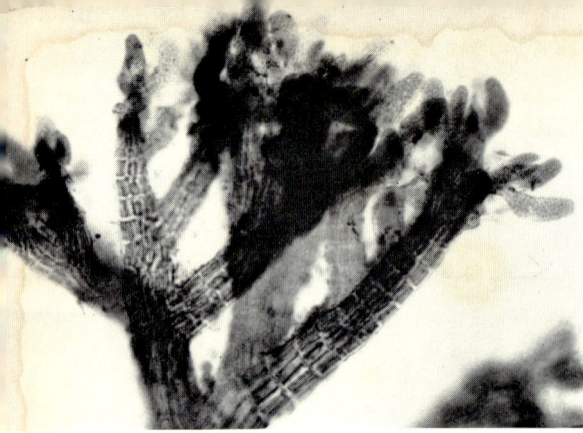

Plate 15. Photomicrograph of the tip of the frond in *Polysiphonia*, showing antheridia. The antheridia are the lightly speckled, club-shaped cells at the top of the picture.

Plate 16. Photomicrograph of a cystocarp of *Polysiphonia*. The polysiphoneous structure of the filament, with its pericentral cells surrounding a main filament, can be clearly seen in this photograph.

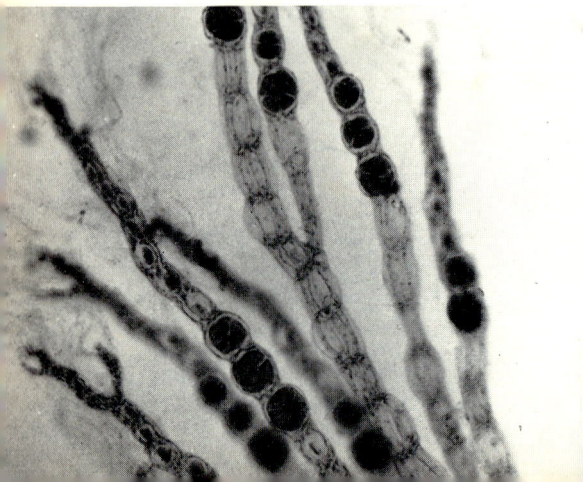

Plate 17. Photomicrograph of tetraspores of *Polysiphonia*.

thoides is widely distributed round British coasts, though it does not occur in sufficient quantities to be rated as common. It is purplish in colour and mucilaginous, and it grows either by itself or in small tufts. Its height is between three and ten inches. It grows from a small holdfast, forming a branched frond about one-tenth of an inch in diameter. It usually occurs attached to rocks or shells in the middle part of the littoral zone, doing particularly well in exposed places. The plant is an annual, and is usually found in Britain from June to October (Fig. 50).

A mature frond of *Nemalion elminthoides* has two layers: a coloured outer portion surrounding a colourless centre. The outer sheath, known as the cortex, is built up of short, branching filaments ending in hairs (Plate 14).

The reproductive organs of *Nemalion* are borne on the lateral filaments. Both male and female organs (antheridia and carpogonia) are formed on the same plant though, since they seldom appear at the same time, it might appear otherwise. The antheridial branches are short, consisting of from four to eight cells only, and each cell is an antheridial mother cell. Each mother cell normally forms four antheridia, each of which contains a single spermatium. After a spermatium has been liberated, another may form in the old antheridium (Fig. 51).

The carpogonial filaments develop from cells near the bases of the lateral branches. At the end of the carpogonial branch is

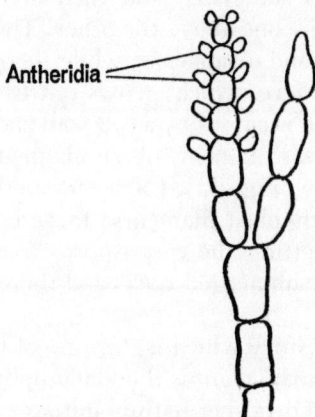

Antheridia

FIGURE 51.
Antheridial branch of Nemalion, *greatly magnified.*

4

FIGURE 52.
Carpogonial branch of Nemalion, *greatly magnified.*

the carpogonium, which has an elongated trichogyne (Fig. 52).

A spermatium drifts against the trichogyne of the carpogonium and lodges there. The nucleus of the spermatium then divides into two, and one or both of the daughter nuclei pass into the trichogyne. One of them travels down into the carpogonium and fuses with the carpogonial nucleus.

After fusion with the nucleus of the spermatium, the carpogonial nucleus enlarges somewhat and then divides into two daughter nuclei, which lie one above the other. The lower of the two nuclei degenerates and disappears, while the upper nucleus travels into a protuberance which grows out from the carpogonium. This outgrowth is cut off by a cell wall and becomes the first cell of a gonimoblast filament, other filaments being later formed in the same way (Fig. 53). Carposporangia are formed at the ends of the gonimoblast filaments; these burst when the carpospores are ripe, setting the carpospores free. The carpospores become fixed to submerged rocks and there develop into new *Nemalion* plants.

Nemalion has a life history which is, for one of the Florideae, extremely simple. The main plant is the gametophyte. Fertilization of the carpogonium by a spermatium initiates the formation of the carposporophyte, which produces carpospores which, in turn, germinate to form a new gametophyte. In most of the

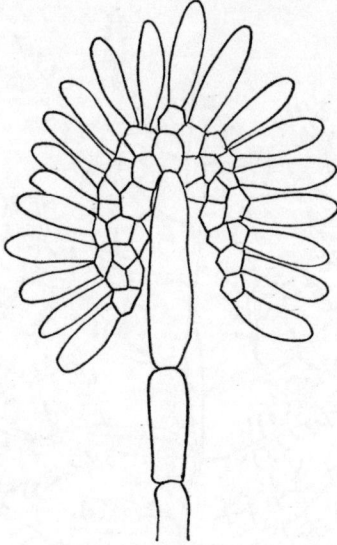

FIGURE 53.
Developing carposporangia of Nemalion, *greatly magnified.*

Florideae there is a second sporophyte generation, the tetrasporophyte, which follows the carposporophyte, but this
complication of the life history is not found in the Nemalionales.

THE GELIDIALES
In the Gelidiales the life history is complicated by the presence
of a tetrasporophyte as well as a carposporophyte. This places
them in advance of the Nemalionales. In spite of this, however,
they are still primitive because the carposporophyte develops
directly from the carpogonium as in *Nemalion*, without the
interpolation of special cells, known as auxiliary cells, such as
are found in the more advanced Florideae.

Gelidium corneum is a common British example of the
Gelidiales. It is an extremely common seaweed throughout the
littoral zone, and is usually found under overhanging rocks and
on the borders of rock pools. It is most abundant in the southern
half of the British Isles, though its range extends as far as the
extreme north of Scotland. The frond has a rigid, rather horny

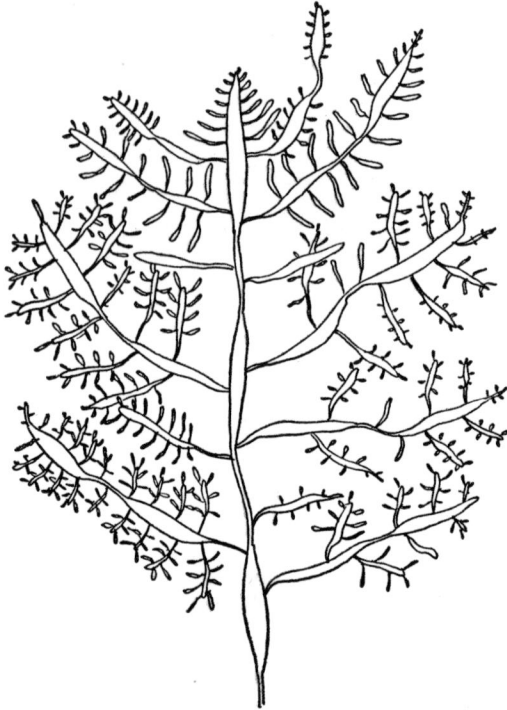

FIGURE 54.
Gelidium corneum.

feel, and is variously coloured from crimson to purple. The frond is forked into flat or cylindrical branches, and it usually grows in close colonies, not unlike a turf (Fig. 54). The fronds are from one to three inches high.

Gelidium corneum is a perennial, the fronds growing up from a persistent basal part each year. When a new frond is growing the first structure to appear is an axial filament formed from a single row of cells. Each cell of this primary filament forms four surrounding cells, called pericentral cells, each of which forms a short lateral filament. Since the tips of the filaments lie close together, the frond has the appearance of a solid mass of tissue.

The male plants of *Gelidium corneum* bear antheridia in groups on fertile lateral branches. A single antheridial mother cell usually produces two antheridia.

The carpogonia are similarly carried on fertile branches, which are usually formed near the growing point. A carpogonial filament generally consists of a single cell which develops into a carpogonium with a long trichogyne. The carpogonium is fertilized by a spermatium brought to it by water currents, and from the fertile carpogonium gonimoblast filaments grow out. The gonimoblast filaments form many one-celled lateral branches, each of which develops into a carposporangium. The mass of gonimoblast filaments is so entangled that one cannot see their origin; probably they arise from more than one fertilized carpogonium, but it is impossible to be certain.

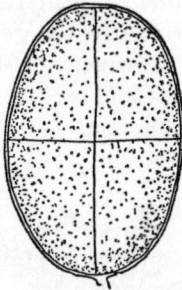

FIGURE 55.
Developing tetrasporangia of Gelidium, *greatly magnified.*

The fate of the carpospores of *Gelidium* has not yet been observed precisely, but it seems impossible to doubt that they give rise to the tetrasporophyte on germination. The tetrasporophyte generation is structurally similar to the gametophyte, but, instead of bearing sex organs on its fertile branches it carries tetrasporangia (Fig. 55). These are sporangia containing four spores each: hence their name. When the tetraspores are liberated it is a fair assumption that they give rise to the gametophyte generation again, though again this has not been fully confirmed by direct observation.

Gelidium is an example of a red seaweed that has three generations in its life history instead of two. The gametophyte gives rise to the carposporophyte, and this is followed by the tetrasporophyte before we get back again to the gametophyte. For those who are interested in the chromosome cycle* the gametophyte generation is haploid, while both the carposporophyte

* See Appendix.

and the tetrasporophyte are diploid, meiosis occurring when the original single nucleus of the young tetrasporangium divides into four to form the four carpospores. Incidentally, this is *not* the case with all the red seaweeds that have three generations in their life histories.

Some species of *Gelidium* are extremely important economically because they are among the chief sources of agar agar. This is a substance which, when dissolved in hot water, sets to a firm jelly on cooling. It is much used in microbiological laboratories for providing a solid medium on which to grow cultures of micro-organisms. The name *Gelidium*, given to the genus by the French botanist Jean Lamouroux more than a century and a half ago, refers to the gelatinous material which can be obtained from the seaweed by boiling in water.

Several other species of *Gelidium* are found on British shores. Some of them are quite common.

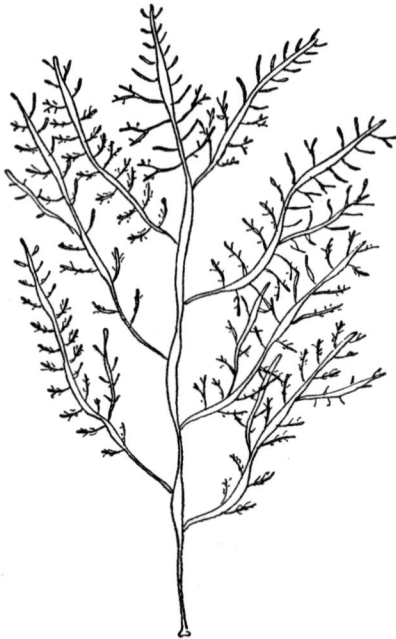

FIGURE 56.
Pterocladia pinnata.

Pterocladia pinnata, formerly known as *P. capillacea*, is the only other member of the Gelidiales which is at all common in British waters. It closely resembles *Gelidium corneum* in appearance, but is a larger and stronger-looking plant (Fig. 56). It usually grows on rocks, and shows a distinct preference for shady situations.

THE CRYPTONEMIALES

The Cryptonemiales are a large order of seaweeds, containing about 85 genera and 650 species. The life history has an additional complication in that the carpogonium does not give rise directly to gonimoblast filaments after fertilization. The

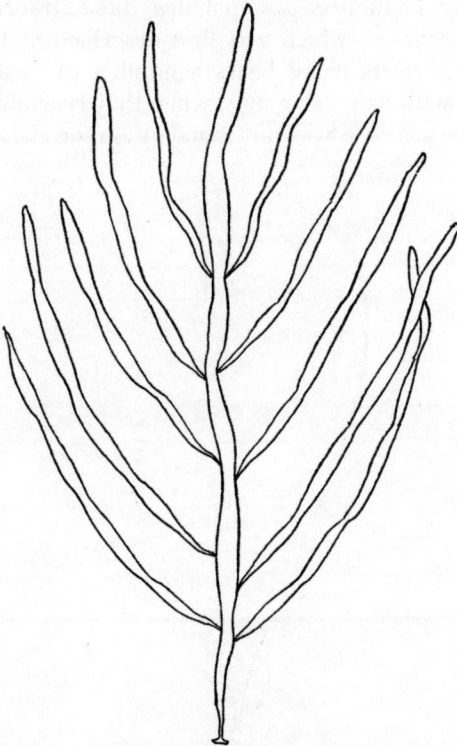

FIGURE 57.
Dumontia incrassata.

fertilized nucleus of the carpogonium, or one of its descendants, migrates into a cell of the filament that bears the carpogonium. This cell is called the nurse cell. A tubular outgrowth from the nurse cell, called an oöblast, then carries the fertilized nucleus to another cell, known as the auxiliary cell, from which the gonimoblast filaments and carposporangia arise.

Dumontia incrassata is a common British species on rocks and stones, usually in the middle of the littoral zone. The fronds vary from purple to yellowish, and are tubular in form, with a main axis, which is usually conspicuous, bearing lateral branches (Fig. 57). The fronds are either solitary or in tufts, and vary in length from one inch to a foot or more.

Dumontia incrassata is an annual plant, and is most abundant in Britain during the spring and early summer.

The family Dumontiaceae includes the extraordinary "sea rose" (*Constantinia*), which was first described in 1768. It was so called because its frond bears a number of "leaves" which become split with increasing age, when they resemble the petals of a rose. The sea rose was not found again for about a hundred

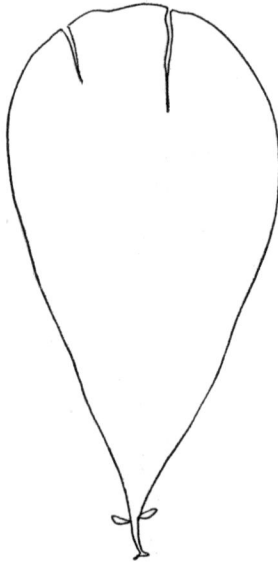

FIGURE 58.
Dilsea carnosa.

years, and many botanists were inclined to doubt its existence until it was rediscovered in the latter half of the nineteenth century.

Another interesting member of the Dumontiaceae is *Dilsea carnosa*, formerly called *D. edulis*. It can be readily recognized by the shape of its frond, which is flat and egg-shaped (Fig. 58), from six to fifteen inches long and from two to five inches wide. The frond is deep red, with a shiny surface, and it springs from a short stipe which is attached to a rock by means of a small holdfast.

Dilsea carnosa grows low down on the shore, where it is only uncovered by the lowest of spring tides. It occurs throughout the British Isles, though it is more common in the south than in the north. It is sometimes wrongly called the dulse, a name that really belongs to another red seaweed, *Rhodymenia palmata*. Although its former name, *D. edulis*, suggests that it is a popular article of food this is not so; although edible, *D. carnosa* has never been widely eaten.

Furcellaria fastigiata (family Furcellariaceae) is a common perennial in rock pools in the lower littoral and sublittoral zones; it grows down to a depth of about fifteen feet. Its fronds are dark red and somewhat cartilaginous, and it forms a small bush about six inches high (Fig. 59). In tetrasporophytic plants

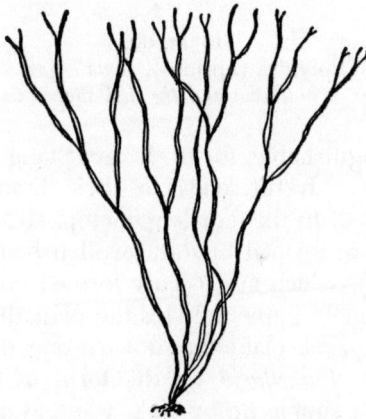

FIGURE 59.
Furcellaria fastigiata.

the branches of the frond end in spindle-shaped pods, distinguishing them from the gametophytes, of which the female plants are shorter, with pods ending in a drawn-out sterile tip, while the male gametophytes have fertile branches ending in oval tips of a yellowish colour.

The only British representative of the family Rhizophyllidaceae is the goat tang (*Polyides caprinus*), a seaweed that can easily be mistaken for *Furcellaria fastigiata*. The goat tang is a perennial plant, from three to six inches high, and of a dull red colour, turning darker when dry. When fruiting the two species

FIGURE 60.
The goat tang (Polyides caprinus), *female gametophyte. Note the swollen nemathecia and the disk-shaped holdfast.*

are easily distinguishable, for in the goat tang the tetrasporangiate plants have fertile ends to their branches which are scarcely thickened. In the female gametophytes the fruit bodies, or cystocarps, are formed in soft, swollen bodies called nemathecia (Fig. 60), which are usually formed on one side of the branch. In the male gametophytes the nemathecia are thin and colourless. When the plants are not fruiting they are best distinguished from *Furcellaria* by the form of the holdfast; in *Polyides* this is a simple fleshy disk, whereas in *Furcellaria* it is divided into a branching mass of rhizoids.

The Corallinaceae are a particularly interesting family of

the Cryptonemiales which have fronds that are thoroughly impregnated with lime and magnesia, making them hard and brittle to the touch: so much so that these odd calcareous seaweeds were originally thought to be corals. It was not until the middle of the last century that it was realized they were seaweeds and not members of the animal kingdom. Their colour is usually pinkish owing to the colour combination of red chromatophores with white lime. Their reproductive organs are carried in flask-shaped cavities called conceptacles, reminding one of the conceptacles of *Fucus*.

The Corallinaceae are extremely important in reef-building in the Pacific Ocean and elsewhere, though the great part they play in the formation of "coral" islands was only recognized at the beginning of the present century. Borings made to depths of more than 1,000 feet on the Pacific island of Funafuti proved that the calcareous seaweeds were more important in the growth of the island than the corals. We know now that many "coral" reefs and "coral" islands in the Pacific are formed mainly, or even entirely, by calcareous seaweeds.

The calcareous red seaweeds are not confined to the tropics, for a number of species are to be found on British coasts. *Corallina officinalis* is a common species on rocky shores all

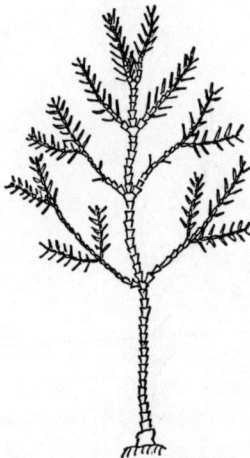

FIGURE 61.
Corallina officinalis.

round Britain, where it is usually to be found on rocks or in shallow rock pools near the low-tide mark. *C. officinalis* appears to enjoy an exposed situation provided it is kept moist; its greatest enemy is desiccation. It is tufted in habit, with a cylindrical frond from one to five inches high, developed from a hard, cylindrical holdfast. The frond consists of segments encrusted with lime; it branches freely, so that its growth is fan-shaped (Fig. 61).

Corallina squamata is another common British species, particularly in southern England and Ireland. It closely resembles *C. officinalis*, so that the two species are difficult to separate. *Jania rubens* is another species which is abundant on the southern coasts of England. It grows in tufts, from half an inch to one and a half inches high, with a beautifully delicate rosy colour. *J. rubens* is usually found growing as an epiphyte on other seaweeds, especially *Cladostephus*, from the mid-littoral zone down to below the low-tide mark. The frond of *J. rubens* is

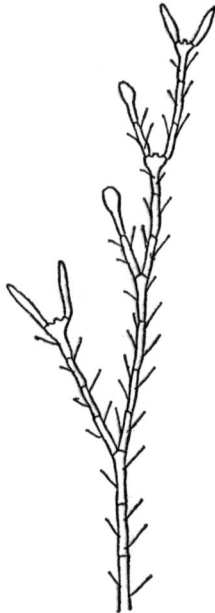

FIGURE 62.
Part of the frond of Jania rubens, *magnified.*

jointed like that of Corallina, but the joints are longer, and only as wide as a piece of thread (Fig. 62).

Lithophyllum encrustans is a common seaweed of rock pools in the littoral zone. It forms a solid crust which may be half an inch or so in thickness, usually with a somewhat irregular surface. Its colour may be anything from rose-violet to yellowish-mauve, varying with the amount of illumination it receives.

Lithothamnion lenormandi resembles *Lithophyllum encrustans*, and is almost as common; it has a distinct preference for shady situations, and is often found growing in rocky crevices and under a covering of *Fucus* on rock surfaces. Its colour is reddish-violet, and it is best distinguished from *Lithophyllum encrustans* by the white margin that surrounds it; this is usually somewhat thickened and lobed.

Mesophyllum lichenoides is somewhat less common than the foregoing species, but it is fairly widespread, especially in the south of England and Ireland. The frond resembles a shell about one inch wide and not more than one-fiftieth of an inch thick. Its colour is rose-pink, and, like *Lithothamnion lenormandi*, it has a white margin.

THE GIGARTINALES

The Gigartinales are an order containing about sixty-five genera and about 500 species. *Gigartina* occurs throughout the subtropical and temperate parts of the Atlantic and Pacific Oceans. During the Second World War it became urgently necessary to find some seaweed that could be used as a source of agar, since the agar-yielding species of *Gelidium* grew in Japanese waters. After considerable research by a team of biologists and chemists set up by the Ministry of Supply *Gigartina stellata* was chosen, not only because it yields a good-quality agar, but also because it is plentiful round the coasts of Britain.

Gigartina stellata grows all round Britain, though it is most plentiful on the west coast. It occurs round about the low-tide mark. It forms thick tufts, from three to six inches high, growing from a disk-shaped holdfast. Its colour is a dark purplish-red. The fronds, which are narrowed at their bases, become ribbon-like higher up, though they seldom reach a width greater than a quarter of an inch (Fig. 63). It is possible to confuse *Gigartina*

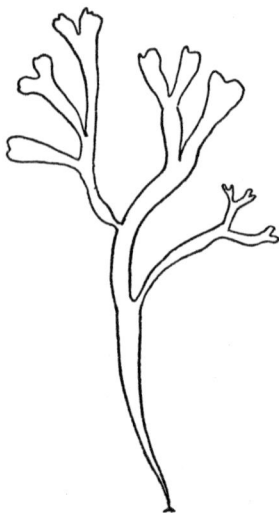

FIGURE 63.
Gigartina stellata.

stellata with *Chondrus crispus* (see later), but the characteristic dark colour of *Gigartina stellata* will usually serve to distinguish it.

There are in all about ninety species of *Gigartina* in the Atlantic and Pacific Oceans. Of these, twenty-eight occur on the Pacific coast of North America, while on the Atlantic coast there is only a single species. The shape of the frond is extremely variable on *Gigartina*; it may be flattened or cylindrical, and either undivided or branched in various ways.

Another member of the Gigartinales that is of economic importance in producing agar is *Gracillaria verrucosa* (formerly called *G. confervoides*). This has a branched, cylindrical frond from six inches to a foot high, attached to a holdfast which is in the form of a fleshy disk that usually bears several fronds. The branching is extremely irregular (Fig. 64). The branches of the gametophyte are studded with large, spherical cystocarps, or fruit bodies resulting from the fertilization of the carpogonia. *G. verrucosa* is a cosmopolitan species; it occurs in Britain, and it is particularly abundant off the coast of South Australia, where it is harvested for making agar.

The best-known British member of the Gigartinales is the

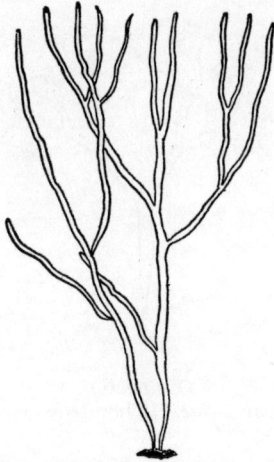

FIGURE 64.
Gracillaria verrucosa.

Irish moss or carragheen, *Chondrus crispus*, a common seaweed on rocks and stones in the littoral zone all round the British coast. It is particularly common on the Irish coast; hence its name. In Ireland it is still used as a food, and in the last hundred years it has become popular as a medicine for coughs and colds. It can also be used for making jellies and blancmanges.

Chondrus crispus is a perennial plant with a flat, ribbon-like frond that branches in a regularly dichotomous manner. Near the holdfast the frond is compressed, but higher up it becomes flat and up to an inch wide, though in some specimens it is narrower. Its colour is a purplish-red (Fig. 65).

THE RHODYMENIALES

The Rhodymeniales are an interesting order in that the frond, which is multiaxial (see p. 90) is hollow, the filaments cut off by the apical cells lying in a circle enclosing a central space.

The best-known British species of the Rhodymeniales is the dulse, or dillisc, *Rhodymenia palmata*. This is a large seaweed, purplish-red in colour, growing in tufts from ten inches to a foot high from a disk-shaped holdfast. The dulse often grows as an epiphyte on the oarweeds of the sublittoral zone, and also

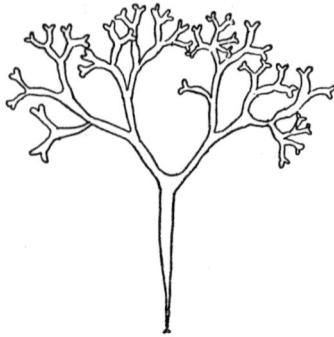

FIGURE 65.
The carragheen (Chondrus crispus)

on the serrated wrack above the low-tide mark; it also grows attached to rocks.

The frond of *Rhodymenia palmata* can be of various shapes, making it rather a difficult species for the amateur to identify. There is hardly any stipe, the frond expanding gradually into a dichotomously branched, flattened blade from a quarter of an inch to one inch in diameter (Fig. 66). The blade is branched, the branching usually being dichotomous, though sometimes it may appear like the fingers of a hand. The final branches may be slightly cleft. The older parts of the frond, which are dark red in colour, usually bear shortly stalked "leaves".

Gastroclonium ovatum is often found in the south of England growing on rocks in the lower littoral zone. It forms bushy plants, from three to six inches high, which are purple or reddish in colour and grow from disk-shaped holdfasts. *G. ovatum* has a tough, cylindrical frond, which is much branched and no more than one twenty-fifth of an inch in diameter (Fig. 67). The branches carry small "leaves", which are actually bladders, and which drop off during the summer, being replaced by others. *G. ovatum* is more frequent in the south of England than in the north, and is rare in Scotland.

The cockscomb, *Plocamium coccineum*, is a sublittoral species, but fresh specimens are often washed up by the tide. It grows in tufts which are from three to nine inches high. The frond is extremely narrow, and is profusely branched (Fig. 68), having

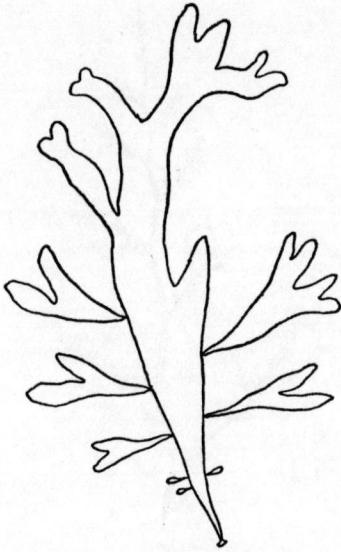

FIGURE 66.
The dulse (Rhodymenia palmata).

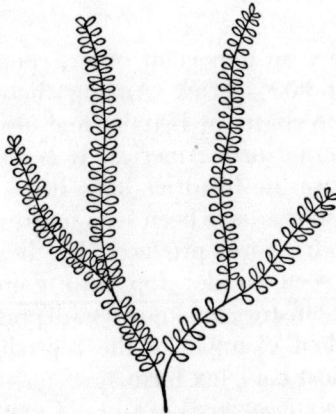

FIGURE 67.
Gastroclonium ovatum.

FIGURE 68.
The cockscomb (Plocamium coccineum).

the appearance in miniature of a branch torn from a tree. *P. coccineum* is particularly attractive when mounted on paper for the seaweed collection.

THE CERAMIALES

The Ceramiales are an important order, containing about 160 genera and about 900 species. Among these, *Polysiphonia* is common round the coasts of Britain, and also on the Atlantic and Pacific coasts of North America. It is also one of the few red seaweeds whose life histories have been worked out completely: the carpospores have been seen to grow into tetrasporophytes, and the tetraspores produced by the tetrasporophytes have also been seen to develop into gametophytes. Since all details of its life history are known with precision, it provides us with an excellent example of the reproduction in the red seaweeds in its most complex form.

The frond of *Polysiphonia*, as in all the Ceramiales, is uniaxial in construction, a central main filament being surrounded by a cortex of pericentral cells formed by the cells of the main axis.

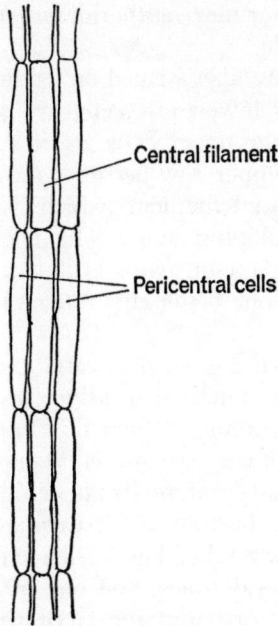

Vertical section of part of a main filament of Polysiphonia, *greatly magnified.*

The number of pericentral cells formed by any one cell of the central axis varies, in different species, from four to twenty-four. The main axis is branched, and the branches are of two kinds: main branches which surround themselves with pericentral cells (Fig. 69), and shorter branches, known as trichoblasts, which do not form a cortex of pericentral cells. The trichoblasts are colourless, or only faintly coloured.

The longitudinal filaments formed by the rows of pericentral cells are called siphons. *Polysiphonia* gets its name from the many siphons that surround the central filament.

The antheridia of *Polysiphonia* are produced by fertile trichoblasts situated near the top of the frond (Plate 15). A fertile trichoblast is usually branched, one branch becoming the short fertile axis, while the other forms a long, branched sterile axis. The fertile axis is unbranched; the bottom two cells remain sterile, while the rest form a cortex of pericentral cells, each of which produces one or more antheridial mother cells which give rise to the antheridia.

The carpogonia are also formed on fertile trichoblasts, which are short; the two lowermost cells are surrounded by pericentral cells while the upper cells are naked. One of the pericentral cells in the upper row becomes the supporting cell that carries the carpogonial filament, which is four cells long, the uppermost cell developing into a long trichogyne. In addition to the carpogonial filament, two sterile filaments are formed on the supporting cell, one being cut off from its base and the other from its side.

A spermatium drifting in the water comes to rest on the trichogyne, and its nucleus, passing down the trichogyne, fertilizes the carpogonium. When this has been accomplished the supporting cell of the carpogonial filament forms a daughter cell, called the auxiliary cell, on its upper side. The auxiliary cell lies just beneath the bottom of the carpogonium, and the two become connected by a tube. The fertilized nucleus of the carpogonium divides several times, and one of the daughter nuclei passes through the tube into the auxiliary cell. Gonimoblast filaments then grow out of the auxiliary cell, their end cells forming carposporangia. In the meantime, the supporting cell, the auxiliary cell, and cells of the sterile filaments join together to form a single large placental cell. The vegetative cells nearby also divide, forming an urn-shaped covering, or cystocarp, which surrounds the gonimoblast filaments (Plate 16).

When the carpospores are set free they develop into tetrasporophytic plants, which resemble the gametophytes. Tetrasporangia are formed from pericentral cells, and in each tetrasporangium four tetraspores are formed, meiosis occurring as the original nucleus of the tetrasporangium divides into four to provide the nuclei of the tetraspores (Plate 17). The tetraspores germinate to form new gametophytes.

Polysiphonia is a large genus, containing some 150 to 200 species (nobody is sure how many), most of which are found in cold or temperate waters, though some grow in the tropics. The lobster horns (*Polysiphonia elongata*) is not uncommon round British coasts. It is a bushy plant, about a foot high, with a branched axis, the branches branching again repeatedly (Fig. 70). The older parts of the frond are dark red while the younger

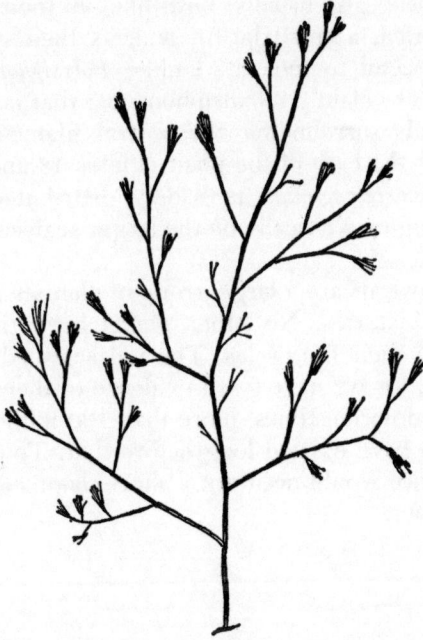

FIGURE 70.
The lobster horns (Polysiphonia elongata).

growth is crimson. It grows at about low-tide level, extending into the sublittoral zone, usually attached to rocks or shells: sometimes it is epiphytic on the larger brown seaweeds. *P. lanosa* is another common British species that grows on the fronds of the knotted wrack, *Ascophyllum nodosum*; occasionally it may be found on *Fucus*. It has fronds about two inches high, which are hair-like in their fineness and branch alternately. *P. urceolata* and P. *brodiaei* are also quite common on British shores.

CALLITHAMNION

Callithamnion is another member of the Ceramiales which has a number of species which occur in British waters, some of them being quite common. The plants are from one to six inches in height, the fronds, as in *Polysiphonia*, being made up of monaxial filaments. These are usually bush-like in their habit (*calli*, beauty; *thamnion*, a small bush), and, as their name implies, extremely graceful to look at. Unlike *Polysiphonia*, plants of *Callithamnion* are mainly monosiphoneous: that is, there are no pericentral cells surrounding the central filament, except, in some cases, at the base of the plant (Plates 18 and 19).

Callithamnion tetragonum is widely distributed in Britain, usually growing epiphytically on the larger seaweeds, especially *Laminaria*.

The red seaweeds are a large group of plants with extremely complex life histories. No other plants have three separate generations in their life cycles. The red seaweeds are also an ancient group, for we have fossil evidence of their existence as far back as Ordovician times, more than 400 million years ago, and they must have existed long before that. To do them anything like justice would need not a short chapter but a book of several volumes.

```
****
* 6 *
****
```

The green seaweeds

By the green seaweeds I really mean the *grass*-green seaweeds, or Chlorophyta, for there are other seaweeds whose colour may be green or greenish but which do not belong here. The chloroplasts of the Chlorophyta contain chlorophyll *a*, chlorophyll *b*, xanthophyll, and carotene, which are the same pigments as are found in the chloroplasts of the higher plants; moreover, the pigments are in approximately the same proportions, which is one reason for believing that the Chlorphyta were the ancestors of the higher plants. At the same time, it would be a fallacy to expect all the Chlorophyta to have the colour of grass, for many of them may appear yellowish or brownish, just as the leaves of flowering plants vary exceedingly in their colour.

The green algae are a large and important group, but few of them are seaweeds; the majority inhabit fresh water or soil. Many of them are microscopic, consisting either of single cells or minute colonies of cells. Others consist of small filaments, just large enough to be seen with the naked eye but requiring the use of a microscope to make out the details of their structure. Some of these microscopic forms are marine, but with them I shall not deal, as they do not fall within the purview of those interested in seaweeds. On the other hand, a few of the Chlorophyta are not only extremely common on the sea shore, but are also large enough to be identified, at least as far as their genera, either at sight or with the use of a hand lens.

THE SEA LETTUCE

The sea lettuce, *Ulva lactuca*, is among the commonest seaweeds ſround British coasts, usually occurring in rock pools in the littoral zone. It particularly favours sea water that is

119

polluted with sewage. It has a broad, thin frond coloured bright green, looking very much like a lettuce leaf. The frond is narrow at the base, where it is attached to the holdfast, becoming wider as the apex is approached. The holdfast is usually attached to a rock or a stone (Fig. 71).

The frond of the sea lettuce is only two cells thick. Each cell contains a single large chloroplast and a single nucleus, the chloroplast being placed towards the outer side of the cell and the nucleus towards the inside.

FIGURE 71
The green laver or sea lettuce (Ulva lactuca).

The sea lettuce has an interesting life history in which there is an isomorphic alternation of generations: the gametophyte and the sporophyte generations are indistinguishable from one another excepting that one bears the sex organs while the other has asexual sporangia. In the gametophyte generation the contents of some of the cells divide up, the nucleus also dividing, so that either thirty-two or sixty-four sex cells, or gametes, are formed. These are released into the water where they swim about, each being provided with a pair of flagella. Eventually they unite in pairs, forming zygotes; since the flagella of each gamete remain distinct, the zygote has four flagella.

At first the zygote swims towards moderate light, but after a time it begins to be repelled by light, so that it tends to swim downwards towards the bottom of the pool. It attaches itself to some solid object and germinates, producing a filament that gradually expands to form the flattened frond of the sporophyte generation.

The spores of the sea lettuce are produced in the same way as the gametes: the contents of some of the cells divide up to form four or eight spores. These resemble the gametes in all respects except in their smaller number and larger size. Each spore has a pair of flagella which enables it to swim, and, like the spores of the oarweeds, it is called a zoöspore on account of its motility. After swimming around for a time the zoöspore germinates and a gametophytic plant is produced.

In the sea lettuce meiosis occurs when the zoöspores are formed. The gametophyte is therefore haploid and the sporophyte diploid.

The sea lettuce is sometimes known as the green laver because it is edible, and is sometimes used as a substitute for the purple laver (*Porphyra umbilicalis*). Although inferior to the purple laver, it is used occasionally at dinner parties. In coastal districts in China it is collected by fishermen and sold either as a food or as a medicine to be used against fevers.

ENTEROMORPHA

Enteromorpha is another extremely common green seaweed. It belongs to the Ulvaceae, the same family as the sea lettuce, and, like the sea lettuce, it has an isomorphic alternation of generations.

The commonest British species of *Enteromorpha* is *E. intestinalis*, so called from a fancied resemblance of the frond, which is a hollow tube constricted at intervals, to a portion of human gut. *E. intestinalis* is abundant in the upper part of the littoral zone, especially where fresh-water streams dash down over the rocks to join the sea. Some species of *Enteromorpha* live in fresh water, and, like *Ulva*, it shows considerable tolerance to waters of varying salinity.

The frond of *Enteromorpha* is constructed in the same manner as that of *Ulva*, consisting of two layers of cells. It differs from *Ulva*, however, in that the two layers, instead of remaining pressed together, are separate from one another, forming a tube about half an inch in diameter. The walls of the tube show slight constrictions at regular intervals (Fig. 72).

FIGURE 72.
Enteromorpha intestinalis.

The life history of *Enteromorpha* resembles that of *Ulva*, except that there is a strong tendency in the genus for the male and female gametes to differ in size; in *E. intestinalis* sexual fusion always takes place between a small male gamete and a large female gamete. In *E. intestinalis* one can distinguish between male and female plants by their colour. The male plants have their fertile parts coloured orange-yellow, while the

THE GREEN SEAWEEDS 123

female plants are coloured yellowish-green in their fertile regions.

There are two other British species of *Enteromorpha*. These are *E. compressa*, which resembles *E. intestinalis* excepting that the frond is branched from the base, forming a tufted growth, and *E. linza*, in which the frond becomes increasingly broad and flattened from the base to the apex, giving the seaweed a strong resemblance to a species of *Ulva*, in which genus the species was formerly placed. The species of *Enteromorpha* are, unfortunately, ill defined, and the range of variation in individual species is great, making it a difficult genus for the beginner.

In China and Japan species of *Enteromorpha* are often eaten, but the habit has not been acquired in the western world.

Enteromorpha has an interesting connexion with the development of wracks on rocky shores. The young plants of *Fucus* seem to do best on rocks which are covered with *Enteromorpha*, forming a soft felt. If it happens that the rocks shelter a large number of limpets (*Patella*), which are strongly addicted to *Enteromorpha*, the limpets eat most of the *Enteromorpha*, which makes it difficult for the fucoids to become established.

CLADOPHORA

Cladophora is an extremely common filamentous green alga, and, unlike most genera of algae, it contains both fresh-water and marine species. The commonest British marine species is *Cladophora rupestris*, which is to be found in large quantities growing on rocks, usually in the lower part of the littoral zone. It often grows beneath the serrated wrack, where it forms a sort of turf. *C. rupestris* forms small tufts of filaments, usually about five inches long, attached to the rocks by short branches which are called rhizoids. The filaments of *Cladophora* are dark green and they branch profusely, giving the plant a feathery appearance (Fig. 73).

The filaments consist of rectangular cells joined together in a row (Plate 20). Each cell has one large chloroplast, which is in the form of a cylindrical network surrounding the cell, inside the cell wall, which has three layers. The inner layer is composed of cellulose, the middle layer consists of pectic compounds, while the outer layer contains a nitrogenous substance that is believed

FIGURE 73.
Cladophora rupestris.

to be chitin, of which the hard outer skeleton of insects is made up.

Cladophora resembles *Ulva* in having an isomorphic alternation of generations. The sporophytic plant produces zoöspores which, unlike the zoöspores of most algae, have four flagella. The zoöspores are formed by the younger cells near the tips of the branches. The zoöspores are liberated from the cells that form them through openings in the cell walls and, after swimming around for a time, germinate to form the gametophytic plants. The zoöspores are usually set free at the time the incoming tide flows over the plants.

The gametophyte of *Cladophora* resembles the sporophyte in all respects. Gametes are produced in the same way as the zoöspores are formed by the sporophyte, but the gametes have two flagella apiece instead of four. The gametes fuse in pairs, and the zygotes so formed germinate to give rise to sporophytic plants.

There are three or four hundred species of *Cladophora*, and the genus is found all over the world.

Spongomorpha is a seaweed closely allied to *Cladophora*, in which genus it was formerly placed. Structurally it is similar to

Cladophora, but it has special filaments which join the main filaments together, producing interwoven tufts which feel spongy to the touch. *Spongomorpha arcta* is a common species round the British shore. It is from two to three inches high, with a slightly blue-green colour. It grows on rocks in rock pools in the lower part of the littoral zone, extending into the sublittoral. It sometimes grows as an epiphyte on other seaweeds. The best time to find it is in the spring or early summer.

Spongomorpha lanosa is a species that grows as an epiphyte. The filaments are shorter than those of *S. arcta*, seldom reaching a length greater than one inch. It is light green in colour, forming tufts that are almost spherical.

THE SIPHONALES

The Siphonales have quite a different structure from the seaweeds so far described in this book. Instead of being divided into separate cells, the whole of the frond forms one vast cell, in which there are many nuclei. Such a structure cannot properly be called a cell: it is usually referred to as a coenocyte.

Bryopsis is a member of the Siphonales. Most of the species occur in the warmer parts of the world, but *B. plumosa* is by no means uncommon round Britain, and the closely related *B. hypnoides* is also a British species, while in North America *B. plumosa* is a common seaweed of the Pacific coast.

Bryopsis plumosa is found on rocky beaches, especially near the low-tide mark, where it is often hidden under ledges of rock. It also grows on the sides of deep pools in the rocks. Although quite common, it is not easy to find unless likely spots are carefully searched.

Bryopsis consists of two parts: a creeping portion that runs over the substratum, and a series of vertical branched filaments. The branches, or pinnae, of the erect filaments bear secondary branches called pinnules, and the whole frond has a feathery appearance (Fig. 74). The erect filaments normally stand from three to four inches high.

Internally, *Bryopsis* consists of one continuous coenocyte from the prostrate filament to the topmost pinnule. The coenocyte is lined with protoplasm containing many small nuclei, and there are numerous small, disk-like chloroplasts (Plate 21).

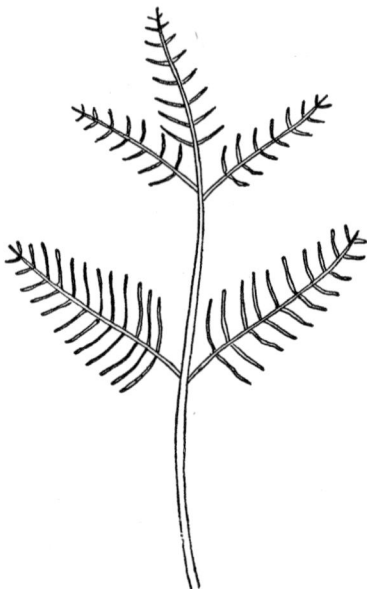

FIGURE 74.
Bryopsis plumosa.

In the centre there is a vacuole. There are no internal cell walls
to divide the coenocyte into cells, except that the older pinnules
develop cell walls at their bases, after which they drop off. The
shed pinnules may develop into new plants.

Apart from vegetative reproduction by the abstraction of the
pinnules, or by the detachment of portions of the prostrate
filament, the reproduction of *Bryopsis* is entirely sexual. Some
of the pinnules become gametangia (structures in which gametes
are formed). The male gametes are small and pear-shaped, with
a pair of flagella at the pointed end. In *B. plumosa*, each has a
single yellowish chloroplast. The female gametes, which are
formed on separate plants, are about three times as large as the
male gametes; again, each gamete has a single chloroplast,
which is bright green. It is possible to distinguish the male and
female plants without the use of a microscope because the male
plants have yellowish fertile pinnules, while those of the female
plants are dark green.

When the gametes are ripe the apex of the fertile pinnule

becomes gelatinous and dissolves away. The male and female gametes fuse, producing zygotes that germinate immediately and grow into a new generation of sexual plants.

In *Bryopsis* no asexual spores are formed, and there is no alternation of generations. The sexual plants are diploid, and meoisis occurs during the formation of the gametes.

In *Bryopsis* the coenocyte is comparatively small and simple, but it is possible for the coenocytic type of organization to give rise to quite complicated structures, such as are found in the family Codiaceae, of which *Codium* is the only British representative. *Codium fragilis* is the largest of the green seaweeds, and is common in deep rock pools in the middle of the intertidal zone of rocky shores, extending down to the low-tide mark. *Codium fragilis* has a much-branched cylindrical frond, about a quarter to half an inch in diameter (Fig, 75), which hangs down from the rocks when uncovered by the tide. The frond is built up of coencytic filaments which are woven together to form a bulky structure. The outside filaments produce a series of swollen, elongated structures called utricles. These contain abundant chloroplasts, and are the organs where most of the photosynthesizing is carried out.

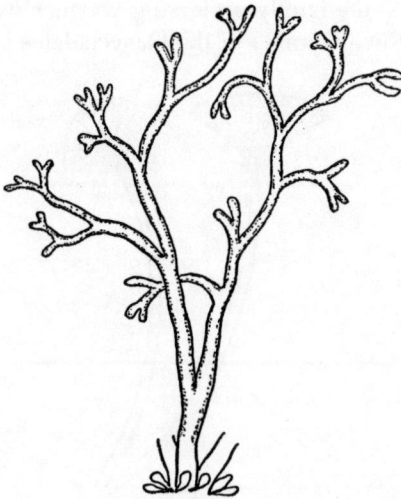

FIGURE 75.
Codium fragilis.

The gametangia of *Codium* are formed on the utricles, one utricle usually bearing two gametangia. The male gametangia form several thousand male gametes, which are small, biflagellate, and each contain two chloroplasts. The female gametangia form several hundred female gametes, which are larger than the male gametes and contain several chloroplasts each. The result of fusion of a male and female gamete is the production of a zygote which grows into a new *Codium* plant. There are no asexual spores, and no alternation of generations.

Codium, like *Bryopsis*, is diploid, meiosis occurring when the gametes are formed.

Codium tomentosum is another British species, very similar to *C. fragilis* and found in similar places. It resembles *C. fragilis* closely, except that its fronds are more slender.

THE DASYCLADALES

The Dasycladales are an interesting order of calcareous seaweeds with a long fossil history; specimens clearly referable to the Dasycladaceae have been found in Ordovician rocks. Their fronds are coated with lime, the outer coating remaining preserved when the soft parts have disappeared. There are no British representatives, the family preferring warmer waters.

The best-known member of the Dasycladales is the mermaid's

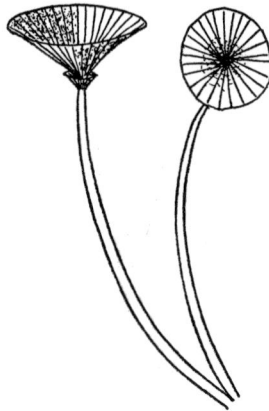

FIGURE 76.
The mermaid's wine glass (Acetabularia).

Plate 18. Photomicrograph of cystocarps of *Callithamnion*.

Plate 19. Photomicrograph of tetrasporangia of *Callithamnion*. Note that the main filament has no pericentral cells.

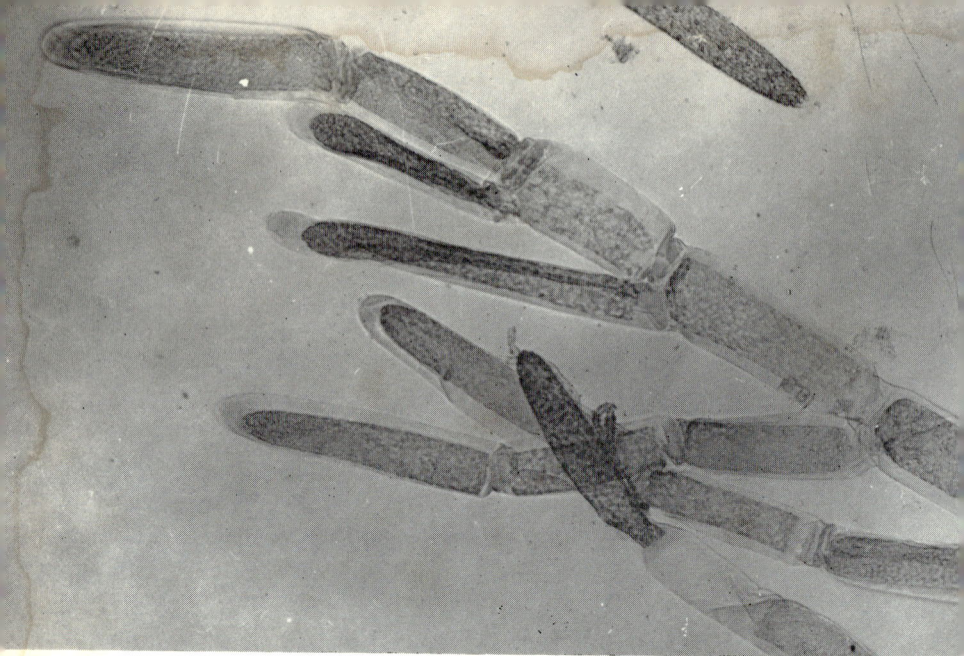

Plate 20. Photomicrograph of tips of filaments of *Cladophora*.

Plate 21. Photomicrograph of tips of filaments of *Bryopsis*. Note absence of cell walls to divide the filaments into separate cells, and the numerous chloroplasts, seen as small dark spots.

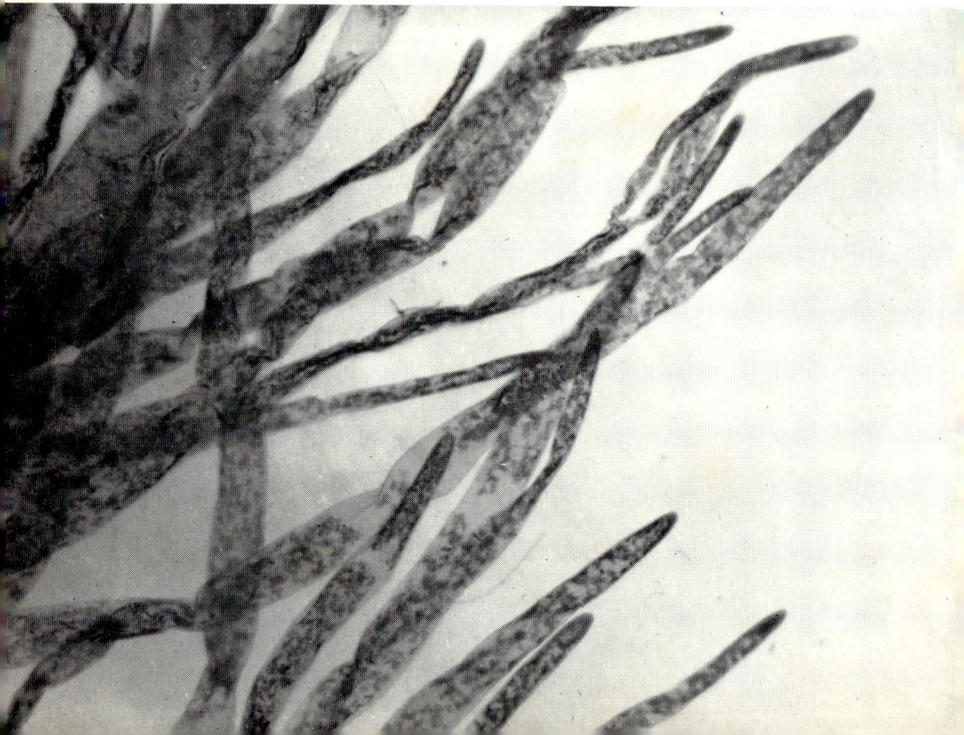

wine glass, *Acetabularia*, which looks something like a small toadstool. It has a slender stem which supports at its tip a ring of branches. In some species of *Acetabularia* the branches are joined together, increasing the resemblance to a toadstool (Fig. 76). The little plants vary from one-fifth of an inch to four inches in height, according to the species. *Acetabularia* is found mainly in the tropics and sub-tropics, but its range includes the Mediterranean.

As in the Siphonales, the Dasycladales, including *Acetabularia*, are coenocytic in structure. They differ from the Siphonales in that, in all species so far investigated, there is only one nucleus. In *Acetabularia* the single nucleus remains at the base of the plant for most of its life, directing the vital processes of the protoplasm by some sort of remote control. Only when sexual reproduction is about to begin does the nucleus divide. It then forms a large number of daughter nuclei which are carried by streaming movements of the protoplasm to the gametangia at the top of the stem.

The Dasycladales used to be included in the Siphonales, but it was felt that their radial structure, and the peculiar behaviour of the nucleus, merited placing them in a separate order.

The Dasycladales are an order which has declined sadly with the passage of time. In former times they were more widespread than they are today, and over sixty fossil genera have been recorded, whereas there are only ten genera living at the present time. *Neomeris*, a genus in which the adult plant resembles a small worm with a tuft of hairs at its apex, is known to have been in existence since Cretaceous times, more than a hundred million years ago. The Dasycladales are a group with an extremely long history behind them; it is to be hoped that they are not heading for extinction yetawhile.

****
* 7 *
****

The blue-green seaweeds

The blue-green algae, Cyanophyta, or Myxophyta are an extremely ancient group of plants. How old they are we cannot say, but they have certainly been in existence for at least a thousand million years, and probably for a great deal longer. Moreover, they have, as far as we know, changed relatively little with the passing of the millennia. They are the most primitive of known plants, and, as might be expected, they have several characters which set them apart from other algae.

One striking difference between the blue-green algae and other seaweeds is that their pigments, instead of being confined to chromatophores, are dispersed through the outer layers of the cytoplasm of the cells. These pigments include chlorophyll a, various carotenes and xanthophylls and, in addition, phycocyanin and phycoerythrin. Since the cells contain red, orange, green, and blue pigments. the possible range of colour of the Cyanophyta is theoretically almost infinite, but in fact their chromatic possibilities are seldom realized. Most of the Cyanophyta are a somewhat dull blue-green.

Another important difference between the Cyanophyta and other seaweeds is the absence of nuclei from their cells. In this respect they differ from all other plants, with the possible exception of some of the bacteria. The central cytoplasm of the cells contains granules, known as metrachromatic granules, some of which at least have been shown to react positively to a chemical test called the Feulgen reaction, showing that they contain chromatin, the characteristic substance found in the nuclei of cells. Presumably, therefore, the metachromatic granules can carry out some of the functions of nuclei.

The Cyanophyta also differ from all other seaweeds except the red seaweeds in that they have no flagellated motile cells in their life histories. Some of the Cyanophyta do possess a kind of motility (see later), but this is of an entirely different type from movement by means of flagella.

The most important characteristic of the Cyanophyta is that sexual reproduction is unknown throughout the group. Most of them reproduce vegetatively; in filamentous forms, for instance, part of the filament may break away and begin life on its own. The unicellular forms reproduce by binary fission, the single cell dividing into two, so that two new individuals are formed. A few of the Cyanophyta may produce spores of a primitive type.

Why sex should never occur in the Cyanophyta is not known. The absence of a proper nucleus may have something to do with it. The main function of sexual reproduction both in animals and plants lies in the fact that in the act of fertilization two nuclei, one from each parent, meet and fuse with one another. In this way the characteristics of both parents are blended in the off-spring, in addition to which, characteristics that are latent in the parents have a chance to become manifest in the new generation. The genes which control the hereditary characteristics of an organism are normally carried in the nucleus; in the Cyanophyta the genes are presumably dispersed with the metachromatic granules, so that their accurate partition, required by the sexual process, would be difficult.

Another point that bears on the lack of sexual reproduction in the Cyanophyta is that they do not appear to possess sterols, the complex organic compounds that are normally associated with sex. Whether this is a contributary factor to their lack of sex, or merely the consequence of it, we do not know.

The cells of the Cyanophyta usually have no vacuoles, and it is thought that this may be one of the reasons that some of the Cyanophyta can withstand extreme desiccation without apparent harm. Some species, however, contain "pseudovacuoles" that are thought to contain gas. These "gas vacuoles" are particularly common in floating species, and it is assumed that the gas gives them buoyancy.

The blue-green seaweeds are all microscopic. Some are unicellular, but usually when cell division occurs the daughter cells do not separate completely, but tend to stick together. Repeated cell-division thus gives rise to a colony. Many blue-green seaweeds have the form of a filament consisting of a single row of cells. A row of cells forming a filament is known as a trichome, and a filament may consist of one trichome or of several trichomes joined together.

The trichomes of many of the blue-green seaweeds are able to move. This movement may consist of a waving motion of the end of the trichome, or the whole trichome may move with a gliding motion. How the trichomes are able to move without flagella is at present something of a mystery, but it is thought that the movement may be due to the secretion of gelatinous matter through minute openings in the cell walls. Some authorities, however, reject this view and consider that the movement is due to waves of expansion and contraction passing along the trichome.

Reproduction in the blue-green seaweeds is either by cell division or by fragmentation. In the unicellular and colonial species the cells divide into two, the two daughter cells separating in unicellular species or remaining stuck together if the species is colonial. In colonial species the size of the colony depends upon how firmly the individual cells are stuck together; if they adhere firmly the colonies grow large, while if they are easily separated the colonies tend to remain small, since as they grow larger, cells break away and form colonies on their own.

In the filamentous blue-green seaweeds the trichomes break up as they grow longer. Many species have large cells called heterocysts, and the break often occurs next door to one of these. Filaments with heterocysts often break down into short lengths called hormogonia; since the hormogonia can move faster than the filaments from which they were formed they soon move away and start to grow into filaments on their own.

Some of the filamentous species give rise to non-motile spores called akinetes, which are cells of the filament that become packed with reserve food material and surround themselves with thick walls. The akinetes are resting spores, designed to enable the seaweed to survive a period when conditions for life are bad. When the conditions improve the akinetes germinate, reproducing the filament.

In some of the blue-green seaweeds the contents of a cell divide up to form a large number of small structures called endospores. Species that behave like this are placed in the order Chamaesiphonales, most of which are marine.

The Cyanophyta are mainly regarded as plants of fresh water and soil rather than as seaweeds, but there are many species that are marine, some of which will be mentioned in Chapter 9.

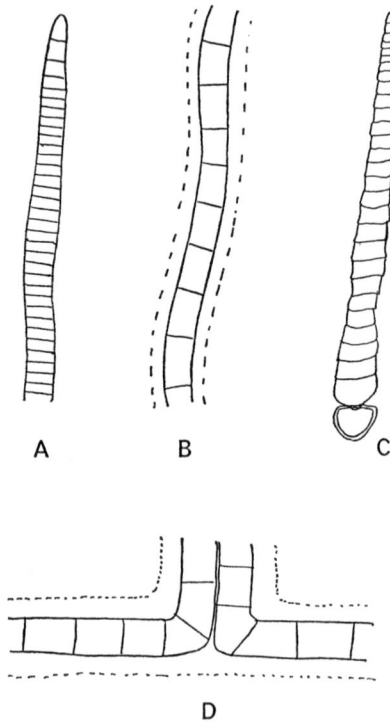

FIGURE 77.
Blue-green seaweeds. A, Part of filament of Oscillatoria. *B, Part of a filament of* Phormidium. *C,* Rivularia. *D, False branching in* Scytonema. *All greatly magnified.*

Oscillatoria is a well-known genus that occurs frequently. It is a filamentous species covered with a thin coating of gelatinous material that is so scanty that it is almost invisible under the microscope (Fig. 77). *Phormidium* is also filamentous, but here the gelatinous outer covering is thick, the filaments being embedded in it to form sheets in which the individual filaments can only be made out by the use of a microscope. *Rivularia* has its trichomes grouped radially, like the spokes of a wheel.

Scytonema shows false branching, a characteristic of certain Cyanophyta. The trichomes are surrounded by a gelatinous sheath; here and there the trichomes split, each portion penetrating the outer sheath and continuing to grow in the same manner as a branch, secreting its own sheath around it.

Pleurocapsa is a species that forms short filaments that creep over the substratum on which it is growing. The filaments produce branches which entangle with one another, so that a flat plate is formed, from which erect branches arise.

Hyella is a rock-penetrating genus in which there is a system of threads spreading over the substratum, with numerous perforating filaments that burrow into the rock. It is found on chalk cliffs, where the softness of the chalk assists the burrowing, and also on the shells of molluscs.

Mastigocoleus is another genus that occurs in the shells of mussels and also in chalk. It has branched filaments, some of the lateral branches ending in hairs.

* * * *
* **8** *
* * * *

The smallest seaweeds

All the seaweeds I have so far discussed, with one notable exception, have been benthic seaweeds: seaweeds that grow anchored by their holdfasts to rocks or other solid objects, or, like the blue-green seaweeds, live in marine soil or form a covering to the rocks or sand on beaches. The exception that I mentioned is *Sargassum*, the floating seaweed from the Sargasso Sea. Since benthic seaweeds live either on or attached to the solid surface of the earth they are confined to a narrow strip of the continental shelf that immediately surrounds the land masses of the world. They cannot live far out in the sea, for as soon as the water gets deep lack of light for photosynthesis makes life impossible for sea weeds.

This does not mean that the open sea is devoid of plant life; far from it, for every pint of sea water all over the world is teeming with microscopic plants. These are the plants that make up the phytoplankton, or free-floating plants that spend the whole of their lives suspended in the water.

The benthic seaweeds are mainly macroscopic forms which are easily visible to the naked eye, though a few, particularly among the blue-green seaweeds, are small, needing a microscope to enable one to make out their structure or, in some instances, to see them at all. The phytoplankton, on the other hand, are all microscopic: very few are even visible to the naked eye.

The reason for this is fairly obvious. To be a member of the phytoplankton the first essential is to be able to float. The smaller an object is, the less is its weight in relation to its surface area.

A simple example will make this clear. Consider a cube of wood measuring one inch along each of its sides. Each face will

5*

have an area of one square inch, making a total surface area of six square inches for the whole cube. Now cut the cube into eight smaller cubes. Each of them will have a total surface area of one and a half square inches, making a total of twelve square inches for the eight smaller cubes. Each of the small cubes will weigh one-eighth of the weight of the original large cube, but its total surface area will be a quarter of the former figure. If we halve the length of side of a cube we reduce its weight by a factor of eight, but its surface area only by a factor of four. I will leave you to work out what would happen to the weight/area ratio if we reduced the length of side of the one-inch cube, not to one-half, but to one-thousandth! That is what we should have to do if we wanted to get chips of wood about the size of organisms of the phytoplankton.

No wonder the phytoplankton can float in the water almost indefinitely. Of course, they would sink to the bottom ultimately if they were left undisturbed, but the sea is never still, even though it may appear so on occasion. Even below the surface there are always small currents, barely detectable, perhaps, but sufficient to keep phytoplankton in suspension.

THE DIATOMS

The chief organisms making up the bulk of the phytoplankton are the minute unicellular algae called diatoms. They belong to the class Bacillariophyceae of the phylum Chrysophyta. The diatoms are well known to every microscopist, whether amateur or professional, for the delicacy and intricacy of the sculpturings on their minute shells not only make them beautiful objects for the microscope, but also serve as a means of testing the performance of optical equipment. The patterns of dots on the shells of *Amphipleura pellucida* or *Suriella gemma*, to name but two, are an excellent test both of the microscopist and the quality of his lenses.

A diatom consists of a single cell enclosed in a shell or frustule. The frustule is composed of two overlapping halves which fit together like a box and its lid. The top half of the frustule is called the epitheca and the bottom half the hypotheca. The parts that correspond with the top and bottom of the box are called the valves, while the pieces that make up the sides of the box are called the connecting bands. The two connecting bands, which overlap one another, form the girdle.

The two valves of a diatom bear a complex system of extremely fine dots—so fine that, in many instances, they tax the resolving power of the microscope to its limit to make them visible. The girdle, on the other hand, is quite plain.

The diatoms may be divided into two main groups: the Pennales and the Centrales. Diatoms belonging to the Pennales are boat-shaped, with the markings on their frustules bilaterally arranged, while those belonging to the Centrales are circular, triangular, or oblong, with radially arranged markings. If seen in girdle view (that is, sideways) the difference between the Pennales and the Centrales disappears, for all diatoms appear oblong in girdle view.

Most of the Pennales have a groove running lengthways down the centre of the frustule, the rows of dots with which the frustule is ornamented being placed on either side of it. This groove is called the raphe. In the middle of the frustule the cell membrane is thickened, forming the central nodule. The raphe dips under the central nodule, running in a minute canal, and reappears on the other side. At either end of the frustule there is another nodule, called the polar nodule, where the raphe ends.

In the Pennales there may be a raphe on both valves, or only on one. If there is only one, it is always on the valve that is normally the lower one, in contact with the substratum. In the Centrales the raphe is absent altogether.

The protoplasm within the raphe is always in a state of streaming motion, and it is thought that it is the friction of the streaming cytoplasm on the substratum that gives the diatoms their power of movement, though movement in diatoms is not yet properly understood.

The frustules of diatoms are highly silicified. Deposits of fossilized diatom frustules occur in various parts of the world. They form the material known as kieselgühr, or diatomaceous earth, which is valuable commercially for a number of different purposes, including packing filters in the sugar industry, and making heat-insulating coverings for furnaces.

The frustule is only the outer covering of the living cell of the diatom. In the cytoplasm are the chloroplasts, which are varied in form. In some Pennales there are one or, more commonly, two large chloroplasts; in other species there are numerous small ones. In some of the Centrales the chloroplasts may be large and lobed, while in others again they may be small and numerous. The latter condition is especially common in marine Centrales.

The pigments contained in the chloroplasts of the diatoms are similar to those found in the brown seaweeds. Besides chlorophyll *a* and chlorophyll *c*, there are xanthophyll, beta-carotene, fucoxanthin, and several pigments related to fucoxanthin. The resultant colour varies from yellow to olive-green or brown. Seen under the microscope the living cells of diatoms glow with a beautiful golden-brown light.

Some of the diatoms form colonies, their cells sticking together in a mass. Where the mass reaches a considerable size it is possible to mistake it for a brown seaweed.

The usual method of reproduction in the diatoms is by cell division. The frustule, which is non-living, does not divide. The original epitheca goes to one of the daughter cells, which grows a new hypotheca to go with it. The old hypotheca goes to the other daughter cell, of which it becomes the *epitheca*, the cell growing a new hypotheca to match it.

It must be remembered that the frustule, being composed almost entirely of hard silica, cannot grow: once a diatom has acquired it the size of the cell is fixed for ever. When a diatom divides the daughter cell that receives the epitheca remains the same size as the parent cell, while the daughter cell that gets the old hypotheca will be smaller (remember that the new hypotheca fits into what is now the epitheca as a box fits into its lid). When this cell divides again, one of its daughter cells will be still smaller, and so on. Consequently, when a population of diatoms is continually reproducing by division, some of the individuals get smaller and smaller.

The logical result of this would be for diatoms to dwindle in size until they finally disappear, but, fortunately for the diatoms and those who enjoy looking at them, Nature has the answer to the problem. Periodically diatoms undergo a process called auxospore formation, which results in the restoration of the diatom to its normal size. Auxospore formation is extremely complex. In most of the Pennales it involves sexual conjugation between two individuals, but in the Centrales this is not part of the process.

Many of the Centrales form microspores, which are minute bodies produced by repeated division of the cell. In some instances the microspores are flagellated, and in at least one species they are thought to be gametes which fertilize another cell which contains a single egg.

Most of the diatoms of the marine phytoplankton belong to the Centrales. Marine diatoms may be of various different shapes. *Coscinodiscus* and *Hyalodiscus*, for instance, are shaped like circular pill-boxes. *Thalassiothrix* and *Asterionella* are long and slender. Sometimes the cells are joined together, forming chains, as in *Guinardia* and *Fragilaria*. The cells may bear spines as in *Biddulphia*, which may be joined together (Fig. 78).

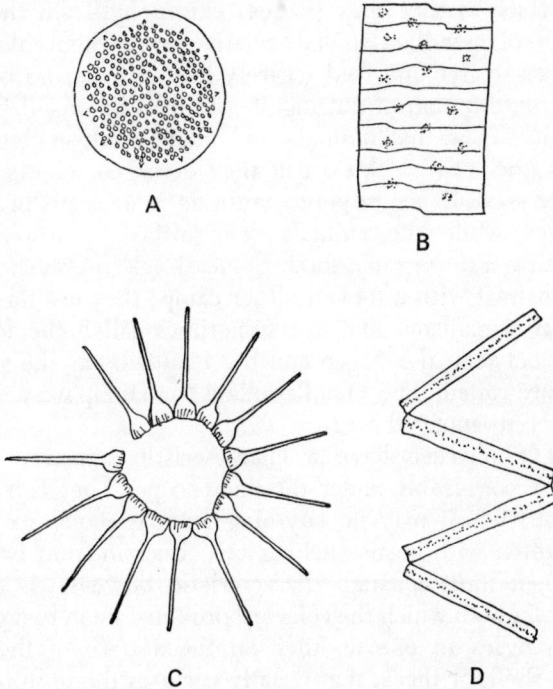

A

B

C

D

FIGURE 78.

Marine diatoms. A, Coscinodiscus. *B,* Guinardia. *C, Colony of* Asterionella. *D, Colony of* Thalassiothrix. *All greatly magnified.*

Diatoms are not all planktonic, for a number of species occur on the sea bottom, or on rocks or sand in the littoral zone. Such diatoms would be classed as benthic.

THE DINOFLAGELLATES

Next in importance to the diatoms in the phytoplankton are the dinoflagellates. These curious organisms belong to the Pyrrophyta (class Dinophyceae), unless one happens to be a zoologist instead of a botanist, in which case one puts them in a group of animals called the Dinoflagellata.

It may sound a little peculiar to classify the same organism as a plant or an animal according to one's point of view, but there is really nothing strange about it. The Dinophyceae (or Dinoflagellata) have certain plant-like attributes, the chief among which is that they possess chlorophyll. On the other hand, some of their dinoflagellate relatives are without chlorophyll and appear to live and feed entirely like animals: no botanist, in fact, would dream of putting these forms among the plants.

The answer is that animals and plants both evolved from common stock. From this stock they diverged, plants for the main part specializing in photosynthesis as a means of feeding themselves while the animals relinquished chlorophyll and henceforth fed on organic food. Some simple organisms, however, remained with a foot in either camp; they are the simple unicellular organisms that are sometimes called the Protista, half-way between the Algae and the Protozoa, as the simplest animals are called. The Dinoflagellata (or Dinophyceae) are to be numbered among these.

The Dinophyceae have a characteristic structure that is instantly recognizable under the microscope. They consist of a single cell, which may be anything from globular to needle-shaped, often with horns sticking out either in front or behind them. Their most constant characteristic, however, is that the two flagella with which the cells are provided lie in two grooves at right-angles to one another on the surface of the heavy cellulose shell, or theca, that usually encloses the protoplasm of the cell. One groove, known as the sulcus, runs fore and aft, while the other, which is called the girdle, runs transversely. The flagellum housed in the sulcus, by its beating, gives the organism a forward movement, while that in the girdle causes it to rotate, though it probably contributes to the forward movement as well.

The pigmentation in the Dinophyceae resembles that of the diatoms and the brown seaweeds. Their chloroplasts contain chlorophyll *a* and *c*, beta-carotene, and a number of xanthophylls, some of which occur only in the Dinophyceae. The freshwater Dinophyceae often store up their reserve foods in the form of starch, which is a typical plant product, but the marine forms nearly always store it up as oil.

Most of the Dinophyceae are enclosed in shells composed of cellulose, though a few are naked. The shell may bear spines.

Reproduction in the Dinophyceae is by simple cell division, and the shell is often shared by the two daughter cells, half going to each. The two parts of the shell do not fit inside one another as in diatoms, so that there is no reduction in size following cell division. Sexual reproduction seldom occurs, though it has been reported for a few species.

The Dinophyceae are most numerous in tropical seas, where they may even outnumber the diatoms, but they are also plentiful in cooler waters. Some, such as *Noctiluca* (Fig. 79), give rise to phosphorescence in the water; in the tropics the light given out by these tiny organisms can be intense.

Sometimes the Dinophyceae increase in numbers to such an

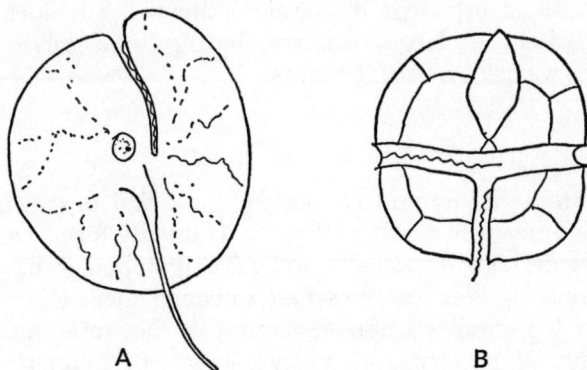

FIGURE 79.
Marine Dinophyceae. A, Noctiluca. *B,* Gonyaulax. *Both greatly magnified.*

extent that they may colour the water. Mention will be made later of *Gymnodinium*, the principal cause of the red tide off the coast of Florida.

OTHER ORGANISMS OF THE PHYTOPLANKTON

The diatoms and the Dinophyceae make up the greater part of the phytoplankton, but certain other organisms are of sufficiently frequent occurrence to require mentioning here. Chief among these are *Halosphaera, Phaeocystis,* and the curious little Coccolithophoridae, all of which are of uncertain systematic position, but are usually placed in the group called the Chrysophyceae, or golden-brown algae, a class of the *Chrysophyta.*

HALOSPHAERA

Halosphaera is large for a member of the phytoplankton, often reaching a diameter of 1 mm. It consists of a single spherical cell containing a vacuole in which a nucleus is suspended by fine protoplasmic threads. Large cells may contain more than one nucleus. The cell contains numerous small, yellowish-green chloroplasts (Fig. 80A).

Halosphaera reproduces asexually by the liberation of numerous zoöspores, each of which has four flagella. As far as we know sexual reproduction does not take place. *Halosphaera* is typically an organism of warmer waters, but it does occur round Britain in large numbers, having been carried into northern waters by ocean currents.

PHAEOCYSTIS

Phaeocystis is an extremely minute, one-celled organism that swims by means of a pair of flagella. It usually forms colonies, the cells dividing repeatedly and sticking together by virtue of the mucilaginous capsules that surround them (Fig. 80B). At times the colonies are so numerous that they make the water feel slimy. Water containing many colonies of *Phaeocystis* repels some animals, notably herrings (see next chapter), causing changes in their paths of migration.

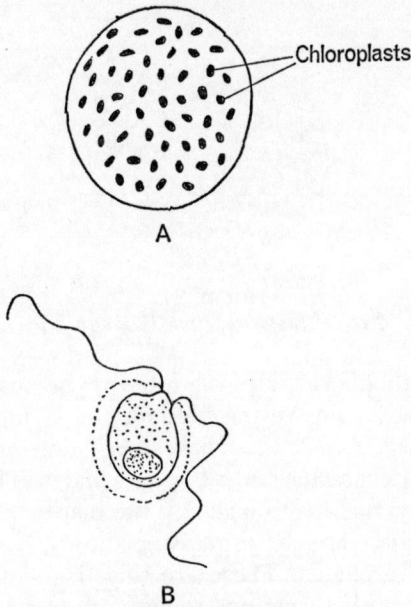

Marine Chrysophyceae. A, Halosphaera. *B,* Phaeocystis. *Both
greatly magnified.*

THE COCCOLITHOPHORES

The Coccolithophoridae are a little-known group of algae
which nevertheless are exceedingly common. They are very
small, and consist of a single spherical cell containing a few
golden-brown chloroplasts. Their most typical feature is the
flat calcareous plates which are embedded in the outer layer of
the cell. Usually these plates consist of oval disks, but in some
species they are ornamented with spines (Fig. 81).

We know very little about the life history of the coccolithophores. Some are non-motile, while others have either two or
four flagella; some are known to have both motile and non-
motile stages in their life histories. Some of the coccolithophores
have a benthic filamentous stage in their life cycles.

The coccolithophores are exceedingly common, and sometimes they occur in such numbers that the water appears milky.
Herring fishermen are of the opinion that the appearance of
"white water" means that herring fishing will be good.

FIGURE 81.
A coccolithophore, greatly magnified.

The coccolithophores are of interest because they were the principal organisms responsible for the laying down of the Cretaceous chalk beds, the chalk consisting mainly of the remains of their characteristic calcareous plates. There are many other organisms that go to make up the marine phytoplankton. In particular, there are the organisms known, from their small size, as microflagellates. These are tiny flagellated plant cells that usually range between one-thousandth of a millimetre and one-fiftieth of a millimetre in diameter. Their life histories are not well known. Organisms without flagella, similar in general appearance to the microflagellates, are also known, as are others which have both motile and non-motile stages in their life histories. In spite of their small size, there can be little doubt that the microflagellates are of great importance as primary producers of organic matter in the oceans.

9

The ecology of seaweeds

Ecology is the study of living organisms in relation to their environment, taking the word environment in its widest possible sense to include not only the physical conditions under which an organism lives, but also the effects on the organism of other living creatures that may be sharing the environment. Ecology today is a rapidly expanding science. A great deal of work has already been done on the ecology of the seaweeds, and especially of the marine phytoplankton which is so important, directly or indirectly, in the food chains of all marine creatures. In this chapter I can do no more than touch on some of the more important aspects of the subject.

In studying the ecology of seaweeds there are two distinct environments to be considered: the littoral zone, and the open sea. By the littoral zone we mean the boundary between the land and the sea, where the nature of the land substratum is of considerable importance in deciding the nature of the seaweed population. In the open sea the nature of the sea bottom is of little or no importance; for the algae that live in the open sea are free-floating and completely independent of the land.

THE LITTORAL ZONE

The word "littoral" is used with different meanings by different people. The littoral zone is commonly taken to mean the region between high and low-tide marks, the terms supralittoral and sublittoral being used to denote the regions above high-tide mark and below low-tide mark respectively. It is in this sense that I used the term earlier in the book. In this chapter I am using the word littoral in its wider sense to include the whole of the region where land and sea meet, from the highest point in a salt-marsh where seaweeds can occur down to the deepest part of the sea where there is enough light to enable seaweeds to grow attached to the sea bottom.

In considering the ecology of the benthic algae—that is, seaweeds that grow attached to the substratum as distinct from pelagic, or free-floating seaweeds—one is immediately struck by the fact that certain ecological factors which are of critical importance to land plants do not apply in the sea. Rainfall and humidity, for instance, which can be matters of life and death to land plants, have no significance for seaweeds which are submerged during at least the greater part of the day. The temperature of the sea is much more constant than that of the land, and the constant composition of sea water is very different from the variability that is found in different types of soil.

On the other hand, there are certain factors in marine life that are not found on land. The disturbance of benthic species of seaweeds by wave action, and the regular periods of emersion of species growing in the intertidal region, are factors which are not found on land.

Although benthic seaweeds grow attached to the substratum, the chemical nature of the substratum does not appear to have any great significance to them. This is in sharp contrast to land plants, which are critically affected by the nature of the soil. For a benthic seaweed the substratum seems merely to provide a point of attachment for the holdfast, the seaweed taking nothing from it, and obtaining all its food elements from the surrounding sea water. On the other hand, the physical nature of the substratum appears, in many cases at least, to be important. Different seaweeds can attach themselves more easily to one type of substratum than another, and thus we find species that show a preference for rock, sand, gravel, or mud.

The temperature of sea water is less variable than the temperature on land, but in some parts of the world the annual variation may still be quite considerable. Along the Atlantic coast of South America, for instance, the annual variation may be as great as 18°C. On the other hand, in tropical seas the annual variation in temperature is usually no more than 2° to 3°C. This variation applies only to surface waters; as you go deeper the variation in temperature becomes less and less. The thermal variation is greater in coastal regions than in the open sea, and may cause a seasonal migration of benthic species to different levels according to the temperature of the water at the time.

The intensity of illumination at different depths in the water naturally has a profound effect on seaweeds, since light is needed for photosynthesis, without which they cannot live. The effects of this, and how the seaweeds manage to get round the difficulty, have been dealt with in Chapter 3.

The pressure exerted by sea water on submerged objects is considerable, and gets greater with increasing depth. At a depth of 330 feet the pressure amounts to about twenty atmospheres, approximately 300 lb. per square inch. Benthic seaweeds have to withstand these high pressures if they live in deep water. In actual fact, the pressure appears to have no observable effect on most seaweeds, with the exception of those species that possess gas bladders. In many bladder-forming species the thickness of the bladder walls becomes greater with increasing depth. If a seaweed is suddenly transferred to a greater depth the gas may be squeezed out of the bladders by the increased pressure, and it may die.

The salinity of sea water is remarkably constant all over the world, although it is somewhat higher in tropical seas than it is elsewhere. The average salinity of salt water is about 35 g. per litre, the greater part of which consists of sodium chloride, or common salt. In the Red Sea the salinity attains a figure of over 40 g. per litre.

These variations in salinity are relatively small, and they appear to have little effect on benthic seaweeds. Where there is a considerable reduction of salinity, as in the mouth of an estuary where fresh water is flowing into the sea, certain benthic species are no longer found, their places being taken by other species. Similarly, in rock pools and lagoons, where sea water becomes isolated and the salinity rises through evaporation, many species of seaweeds are prevented from growing.

Some seaweeds, such as certain species of *Enteromorpha*, can tolerate a wide range of salinity, and they may prefer to grow in water with a salinity differing from sea water. The common *E. intestinalis* grows best in slightly diluted sea water, but it is perfectly capable of growing in fresh water, brackish water, or sea water, and it will even tolerate a solution of brine.

The effect of wave action on seaweeds is considerable, as may be seen if the seaweed flora of a sheltered bay is compared with that of an exposed headland. In the bay the shore is to some extent protected, while the headland is fully exposed to the fury of the elements. The total effect of wave action is complex. On the headland the action of the waves may prevent the spores of seaweeds from fixing themselves to the rocks, or the fragile sporelings that have been produced from spores that have managed to find lodgement may be torn away before they have had time to grow into seaweeds. On the other hand, in the less turbulent water of a sheltered bay the calm water may allow a deposit of mud to be formed on the rocks; this may be a bar to some species of seaweeds, while others may find it an advantage.

The pH (that is, the acidity or alkalinity) of sea water is usually slightly on the alkaline side, the pH varying between 7·9 and 8·3 (pure water, which is neither acid nor alkaline, has a pH of 7; pH numbers above 7 indicate increasing alkalinity, while a value below 7 indicates acidity). The slight alkalinity of sea water is explained by the fact that most of the carbon dioxide it contains in solution is in the form of carbonates and bicarbonates. The photosynthetic activities of seaweeds, removing carbon dioxide from the water, cause bicarbonates to dissociate, thus making the water more alkaline. In rock pools which contain actively photosynthesizing seaweeds such as the sea lettuce the pH may rise as high as 10 in the course of a few hours. Some seaweeds cannot stand water as alkaline as this. Where the sea lettuce is plentiful in a rock pool it often suppresses the growth of other seaweeds, especially red seaweeds.

The effect of the tide on the seaweed population of a shore is profound; probably greater than any other single factor. This is seen on the phenomenon of zonation, which I have already mentioned in connexion with the brown seaweeds. Zonation may be observed on any rocky shore anywhere in the world: some species of seaweeds grow high up on the shore, while others prefer a position lower down, nearer to the sea.

Zonation is seen at its best on a gently sloping rocky beach, where the different zones are so spread out that they are obvious to the eye. Zonation does not depend, however, on a large tidal rise, for it can be seen clearly in the Caribbean where the mean tidal rise is often no more than nine inches. It reaches its best development on the colder Atlantic shores of Europe.

The effects of tidal rhythm on the reproduction of such seaweeds as *Dictyota dichotoma* has already been dealt with. We are still a long way from understanding how this rhythm becomes implanted on the seaweeds.

The littoral region in its wider sense may be subdivided into sub-regions or zones. For instance, we can distinguish readily between the three major zones where seaweeds are permanently submerged by the sea water, regularly covered and uncovered by every tide, and above the normal high-tide mark, so that they are only reached by the highest spring tides. Each zone has its particular characteristics. Most of the work that has been done on the ecology of benthic seaweeds has been on the intertidal zone, where there are two periods of submersion and emersion every twenty-four hours, but recently the other zones have been coming in for more attention.

THE SUPRATIDAL ZONE

This is the zone above high-tide mark, and the seaweeds capable of inhabiting it vary very much with the nature of the substratum. If the beach is sandy it will almost certainly be too dry for much colonization by seaweeds, and they will only occasionally be found. If soil containing organic matter stretches down to the high-tide mark, however, conditions will be a little more promising, especially for microscopic forms such as diatoms. *Nitschia obtusa*, for instance, is a diatom often found in marine soil.

Where the substratum is composed of rock, seaweeds will be more plentiful. Besides relatively large seaweeds such as the channelled wrack and the purple laver, there is likely to be quite a rich flora of microscopic forms. In particular, many species of blue-green seaweeds are likely to be found, often forming a black covering to the rocks. Among others, species of *Oscillatoria*, *Phormidium*, and *Rivularia* are common in this zone.

The blue-green seaweeds may show their own zonation in the supratidal zone. This is especially noticeable on the shores of the Adriatic, particularly where the rocks are calcareous. The highest zone above the tide mark may be occupied by *Pleurocapsa* and *Scytonema*. As we approach the sea, a zone containing

Mastigocoleus may be found, and finally, as we near the high-tide mark, there is a zone containing species of *Hyella*.

The same kind of thing may be seen on chalk cliffs. The highest seaweed community usually contains the green seaweed *Endoderma perforans*, a primarily filamentous form in which the filaments may coalesce to form a sheet one cell thick. Below this zone we tend to find microscopic Chrysophyta, such as *Gloeochrysis maritima*; blue-green seaweeds may also occur here. The lowest zone, frequently splashed by sea water at high tides, consists mainly of species of *Enteromorpha*, but this zone is frequently infiltrated by seaweeds from the zones above and below it.

THE INTERTIDAL ZONE

The intertidal zone lies between high and low-tide marks, where the seaweeds are subjected to periodical covering and uncovering by the tides. To see the larger seaweeds at their best one must go to a rocky shore, for most of them are rock inhabitants.

The intertidal zone is frequently subdivided into three sub-zones. In the upper zone the seaweeds are exposed for most of the time, being covered only for short periods when the tide is up. In the middle zone, which is usually the most extensive, the seaweeds are well covered by each tide, but they are also exposed when the tide drops. In the lower zone the seaweeds are only uncovered for short periods at low tide. The three zones correspond roughly with the zones usually occupied by the channelled wrack, the bladder wrack, and the serrated wrack respectively, but there is considerable overlapping, and the seaweeds of the intertidal zone spread into the supratidal and subtidal zones. However, the three sub-zones can be recognized on most rocky shores all over the world.

On British shores the most conspicuous species of the upper sub-zone are the channelled wrack and the spiral wrack, the spiral wrack often somewhat below the channelled wrack, and the purple laver. Smaller species occupy cracks in the rocks, and there are usually plenty of blue-green seaweeds and diatoms among the microscopic flora. Where a fresh-water stream flows over the rocks species of *Enteromorpha* are often found.

In the middle sub-zone round Britain the larger seaweeds consist chiefly of the bladder wrack, the toothed wrack (towards the lower edge), the knotted wrack, carragheen (*Chondrus crispus*), and, again towards the lower edge, *Gigartina stellata*. The fronds of the knotted wrack often bear a dense covering of *Ectocarpus*, *Ceramium*, and *Polysiphonia*. The rock pools bear a rich flora of red seaweeds, and the brown seaweeds *Halidrys siliquosa* (the sea oak) and *Lomentaria articulata*.

If the shore is exposed to extreme wave action the flora of the middle sub-zone may be severely curtailed or even absent altogether.

The lower sub-zone consists of a band just above the level of the low-water mark, so that the seaweeds inhabiting it may be exposed only for a few minutes at each low tide. Around British coasts the most important species of the lower intertidal sub-zone are species of Laminariales, such as the tangle, the cuvie, and the sea belt. In this zone we also find the sea thong, species of *Codium*, and various red seaweeds. We may also find seaweeds characteristic of the middle sub-zone, especially in rock pools.

Throughout the intertidal zone we often find the larger seaweeds covered with a dense coating of smaller epiphytes. These may consist of filamentous representatives of the brown, red, and green seaweeds, and also microscopic blue-green seaweeds and diatoms. The diatoms and smaller blue-green seaweeds may grow on the larger epiphytic species such as *Ectocarpus* and *Polysiphonia*.

THE OPEN SEA

Although the large benthic seaweeds form the most obvious element in the marine flora, they are only a part—and a small part—of the total flora of the sea. Greater by far in numbers, and also in importance—are the floating microscopic algae that make up the marine phytoplankton.

The oceans cover about seventy-one per cent of the surface of the earth, and the number of these tiny organisms contained in the seas defies imagination. They are present everywhere, from the Equator to the Arctic and Antarctic regions. Although they are so small, the organisms of the plankton make up in numbers what they lack in size. If they could be weighed they would be found to weigh more than all the other plants of the world put together.

The biological significance of the phytoplankton is almost incalculable, for they are the primary food of everything that lives in the sea. In particular, they nourish the copepods and other small animals which in turn are eaten by many kinds of fish. Just as on land one may say that all flesh is grass, since even the most extreme carnivores such as the cats must eat other, herbivorous animals, so might one say that in the sea all flesh is plankton.

The marine plankton owes its particular importance to the fact that it is photosynthetic: it can build up its substance from carbon dioxide and mineral salts, which are purely inorganic sources. Only plants can do this. The organisms of the marine plankton, therefore, are the primary producers of the oceans. On the organic matter that they conjure out of the air all animal life in the sea must ultimately depend.

The importance of the plankton does not rest on this alone. It also plays a part in biogeochemical reactions between the seas and the atmosphere above it. It is a remarkable fact that, at any rate until recently, the carbon dioxide content of the atmosphere has remained constant at about 0·03 per cent. This is largely due to the oceans acting as a buffer, giving up carbon dioxide to the atmosphere if the atmospheric content falls a little, and absorbing carbon dioxide should there be a surplus. In this important buffer action the activities of the marine phytoplankton play a significant part.

The marine phytoplankton consists largely of diatoms and dinoflagellates (Pyrrophyta), with some blue-green algae and unicellular green algae. Associated with them are countless numbers of even smaller organisms that make up the fraction of the phytoplankton known as the nannoplankton (Latin, *nanus*, a dwarf). The nannoplankton, which includes the curious organisms called coccolithophores, has been comparatively little studied until recently, largely owing to the difficulties encountered in attempting to collect such small creatures from the sea.

The traditional method of collecting samples of planktonic organisms is by means of a plankton net. This is a net of fine mesh at the base of which is a tube in which most of the plankton collects. The mouth of the net, which is usually from a foot to a yard in diameter, is held open by a hoop, to which the three cords or bridles attaching the net to a tow rope are fixed. The net is towed through the water at a slow speed; slowness is important, because if the net is towed too fast it sets up turbulence in the water that deflects floating objects, including plankton, away from the mouth. After towing for a specified time the net is raised, the collecting tube removed, and the net itself washed into a bowl or other receiver to collect any planktonic organisms that may have stuck to the net instead of passing down into the tube at the end.

A plankton net is not really a very efficient means of sampling the plankton, for it only collects from one to ten per cent of the plankton in a sample of water. If the mesh of the net is too fine the turbulence set up on towing it through the water deflects much of the plankton clear of the opening of the net. On the other hand, if the mesh is too coarse, though there is far less turbulence, much of the smaller organisms will pass through without being caught. For collecting organisms of various sizes it is a common practice to use three nets with different size mesh.

Plankton nets are usually made of bolting cloth. This may be of silk or nylon. Bolting cloth is used industrially for sieving flour or other material, and its particular feature is that, by the way in which it is woven, its mesh remains practically constant even when under strain. The three grades commonly used for making plankton nets are numbers 3, 15, and 21, corresponding to mesh sizes of 0·324, 0·0925, and 0·063 mm. respectively.

Many modifications of the simple plankton net have been tried in order to get increased efficiency of filtration. One simple modification is the Hansen net, where a canvas sleeve surrounds the opening (Fig. 82), the sleeve having an opening a trifle smaller than that of the net proper. The Hansen net is a little better than the simple form of plankton net, but still leaves a great deal to be desired.

Organisms of the nannoplankton will pass through even the finest net, so that other means have to be adopted in order to extract them from sea water. These methods usually depend on concentrating the plankton in some way. The simplest

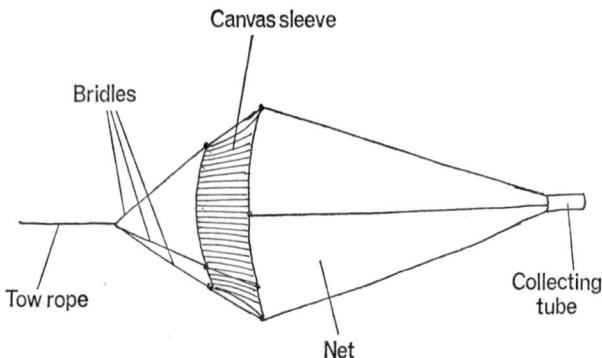

FIGURE 82.
The Hansen net for collecting plankton.

method is to allow a sample of the sea water to stand undisturbed, when the planktonic organisms will tend to settle towards the bottom. Alternatively, the settling may be artificially accelerated by centrifuging—that is, placing the sample of sea water in an instrument somewhat resembling a cream separator, in which it is whirled round at several thousand revolutions a minute. A third method is to filter the sea water through a membrane filter.

An alternative to towing a plankton net through the water is to sink it to a given depth and then raise it slowly. This has the same effect as towing the net behind a boat, with the advantage that plankton from different depths is obtained.

It is sometimes desired to take plankton samples from a given depth in the water, to compare it with samples taken from other depths. The problem here is to close the mouth of the plankton net before raising it, so that the sample will not be contaminated with plankton from higher depths as the net is raised. Various modifications of the net have been devised to enable this to be done. The simplest is the Hansen net, in which the mouth is fitted with a noose which can be drawn tight, thus closing the mouth before the net is pulled up. Other nets, such as the Clarke-Bumpus net, have their mouths fitted with valves which can be opened or closed by a "messenger"—a moderately heavy object which slides down the rope that tows the plankton net and operates the valve mechanism.

Quantitative plankton measurements—the measurement of the amount of plankton in a given volume of water—are difficult. For one thing, it is extremely hard to estimate exactly how much water has been filtered by the net, since some of the water is almost certain to have been displaced by turbulence. In accurate quantitative studies a flow meter is usually incorporated in the mouth of the net. This consists of a propellor with several blades, which is connected with some form of revolution counter. By the number of revolutions the propellor has made during the operation it is possible to calculate with fair accuracy how much water has passed through the net. There is still the problem, however, of small organisms passing through the meshes of the net and so escaping.

In recent years high-speed plankton counters have been developed, which offer some advantages over the plankton net. For one thing, a plankton net must be towed slowly, which means that it can only be used from a boat that is being operated for the purpose of collecting plankton. A high-speed plankton sampler can be operated at reasonable speeds, and so can be towed behind a vessel during a commercial voyage. Another advantage of the high-speed plankton samplers is that they are said to have greater efficiency in capturing actively swimming specimens that might otherwise escape.

The main feature of a high-speed plankton sampler is that the area of the net is large compared with the mouth of the sampler, reducing turbulence when the apparatus is towed rapidly through the water. The simplest arrangement is found in the Hardy plankton sampler, which is a metal cylinder shaped rather like a torpedo. There is a small opening in the nose through which water enters the plankton net, passing out through another opening at the rear end of the device. The body of the plankton sampler is fitted with stabilizing fins.

A somewhat similar, but larger, plankton sampler known as the Gulf III sampler, incorporates a flow meter in the rear opening. The Gulf III sampler has been used fairly recently for making surveys of the plankton round Britain.

Perhaps the most sophisticated plankton sampler so far devised is the Hardy continuous recorder, designed to give a record of the plankton distribution over a long distance. This apparatus has a propellor, driven by the movement of the apparatus through the water, which draws a strip of bolting cloth slowly across the path of the water entering the device. Plankton trapped on the cloth are retained in their original places by another strip of cloth applied to the first, and the two pieces of cloth are wound up together in a tank of formalin, as a plankton preservative. At the end of the operation the spool of cloth is unwound and the positions of the planktonic organisms noted. From this it is possible the chart the position in the sea of any portion of the sample by reference to the ship's log.

The composition of the phytoplankton varies widely in different parts of the world. Some common species are world-wide in their distribution, but others are confined to certain waters. There are many currents in the oceans, both large and small; the well-known Gulf Stream is only one of them. The water in each current has its own special chemical attributes, and the physical characteristics—temperature and so on—also vary in different currents. As a consequence, the phytoplankton found in each current varies in its species composition. There are, for instance, separate Arctic and Antarctic species, in spite of the apparent general similarity between the climatic conditions that prevail in the two environments.

The marine phytoplankton is often split into two main types: the neritic phytoplankton occurring round coastal areas, and the oceanic phytoplankton which is characteristic of the open sea. The neritic phytoplankton often contains species that are not truly planktonic, but have been washed out of communities whose home is the littoral region. Water near the coast usually contains a higher nutrient content, especially of organic matter, than the open sea, and this has an effect on the neritic phyto-plankton, supporting the growth of species that might find it difficult to survive in the open sea. The increased turbidity of inshore waters also probably has an adverse effect on oceanic species of phytoplankton. The neritic phytoplankton usually contains a higher proportion of species with highly silicified shells. Such shells are heavy, and species having them tend to sediment out of oceanic waters, whereas the greater turbulence of coastal seas helps to keep them in suspension.

Although the marine phytoplankton usually pass unnoticed owing to their small size, they can at times make themselves very noticeable indeed. Water blooms—the sudden increase in number of planktonic algae—are a common phenomenon in fresh water, and they can also occur in the sea. For example, the water of the North Sea periodically takes on a muddy appearance known by fishermen as "baccy juice". This phenomenon is due to the occurrence of vast numbers of a tiny marine flagellate called *Phaeocystis ponchetii*. This organism is repulsive to herrings. In the spring, *P. ponchetii* often makes its appearance off the coast of Holland, and because of it the northbound herring migration is turned to the west, so that the East Anglian herring fisheries benefit. Occasionally, as in the year 1927, there may be an abnormal increase of *P. ponchetii* out of season. When this happens, the southern migration of the herrings may be altered; the effect of this on the herring fisheries is quite unpredictable.

Another instance of a marine water bloom occurs from time to time off the coast of Florida, and is known locally as the Red Tide. The sea water is turned red by the occurrence of enormous numbers of a red dinoflagellate called *Gymnodinium brevis*. This organism is pigmented; hence the red colour imparted to the water, which also feels soapy to the touch.

The effects of the Red Tide are most unfortunate. Fish that swim into the Red Tide are killed, and their bodies are washed up on the coast of Florida in their millions, poisoned by a toxin that is given off by the Red Tide organism. Bulldozers have to be used to rid the shores of the bodies of the poisoned fish. Porpoises and turtles are also poisoned, as are sea birds and shore organisms that eat the poisoned fish. Shellfish are also affected, so that it becomes dangerous to eat clams or oysters.

Besides the danger of poisoning, a gas is given off by the organism which, when carried by the westerly wind to the shore, causes people to cough and sneeze intolerably. The local citizens' committee is constantly asking the State of Florida to sanction grants for research into the causes and eradication of the Red Tide, and as constantly complaining of the "chamber of commerce" mentality of a certain section of the community who tend to minimize the effects of the Red Tide lest undue publicity should spoil the tourist trade.

The condition favouring an outbreak of Red Tide seems to be heavy summer rains. These wash down millions of tons of fresh water into the Gulf of Mexico, and this water is held inshore by the prevailing westerly winds. At the same time the water is fertilized by phosphates carried down by rivers from the phosphate mines of Central Florida, making matters worse. More than five thousand different chemicals have been tried by the Bureau of Commercial Fisheries to get rid of the Red Tide but so far none has proved to be entirely satisfactory.

*****
10
*****

How seaweeds are used

Seaweeds are more useful than most people realize. Apart from the vast importance of the marine phytoplankton, which supports all other life in the sea, there are numerous ways in which seaweeds are useful to man.

The oldest use to which seaweeds have been put was their use as food for man and beast. Nobody knows exactly when phycophagy—the eating of seaweeds—began, but it must have been before the dawn of history.

In the western world seaweeds are not popular as food, the only one that is regularly eaten being the purple laver, *Porphyra umbilicalis*, though others, such as the green laver, *Ulva lactuca*, and the carragheen, *Chondrus crispus*, occasionally appear on the menu. In the East, and particularly in China and Japan, some seaweeds are highly sought after as articles of food. Malaya and the South Sea Islands are also centres of phycophagy.

It is thought that the cultivation of seaweeds for food began in Hawaii, and today the Hawaiians commonly eat about seventy different species. It used to be the custom long ago in Polynesia for villages to be built close to the sea, and the more wealthy villagers used to cultivate marine gardens where they grew edible seaweeds. In Japan seaweed "farms" are common, *Porphyra tenera* being the species most commonly grown. The method of cultivation on bamboo poles has already been described. It is said that *Porphyra* plants raised by the Japanese method are larger and more tender than those occurring naturally.

Another Japanese food, called Kombu, is prepared from the larger Laminariales, particularly *Alaria*, *Arthrothamnus*, and *Laminaria*. The seaweed is collected, usually from open boats, using specially designed hooks. It is then dried and cut up, and

6

161

according to how the cutting is carried out one can get shredded kombu, pulpy kombu, sweet-cake kombu and so on. In 1936 nearly three hundred thousand tons of wet seaweed were harvested for making various kinds of kombu.

Other seaweeds are used as food in Japan from time to time. The foods prepared include Arame from *Eisenia bicyclis*, Hijiki from *Hijikia fusiforme*, Miru from a variety of seaweeds, including *Codium*, and Wakame from *Undaria pinnatifida*.

Whether or not these seaweeds are of any great nutritional value is open to doubt. The Japanese *Porphyra* and an edible blue-green alga called *Nostoc* that is eaten in China both have a high nitrogen content, and so must be presumed to be fairly nutritious. The other seaweeds no doubt supply carbohydrate, and the iodine that most of them contain is probably of some value in preventing goitre, a disease caused by lack of iodine in the diet. Certainly goitre does not appear to be common in countries where seaweeds are extensively eaten. The vitamin content of many seaweeds is high, and this adds to their value as food. Probably the chief value of seaweed in the diet is to add roughage to what is eaten in countries where the staple foods are rice and fish.

For centuries seaweeds have been used as fodder for animals on farms near the coast. Seaweed makes an excellent fodder for farm beasts, for animals appear to be able to digest it better than human beings can. In one of the Orkney islands seaweed is the sole food of a race of sheep, who appear to thrive on it. The larger brown seaweeds are used, especially *Fucus* and *Ascophyllum* and, to a lesser extent, *Laminaria*.

On the Continent they have even gone so far as to set up factories to manufacture meal from seaweeds for feeding stock, and it has been found that the seaweed meal is as nutritious as normal cattle foods such as hay. The laminarin contained in the seaweeds appears to be the chief source of nourishment, and it is therefore important to harvest the weeds at the time when their laminarin content is at a maximum.

Besides the use of seaweed for the feeding of stock, the large brown seaweeds have extensively been used as a manure for the land. The best method of using seaweed as manure is to plough it in while fresh, but it can be left on the surface of the soil to rot down, or made into compost with other materials. Seaweed has a high nitrogen and potash content, but is rather low in phosphorus. It takes some time for the nitrogen in seaweed to become available to plants, so that seaweed is a manure of the slow-acting but long-lasting kind.

It is particularly valuable in supplying some of the trace elements: substances that plants need in extremely small quantities but which are nonetheless essential to healthy plant life.

Members of the Corallinaceae, such as *Lithothamnion*, contain a great deal of lime in their fronds, and where they are especially plentiful—as in the Hebrides, Connemara in Ireland, and Cornwall—they have given rise to what are called "coral sands". These coral sands are used as lime dressings for the land, valuable where the soil is inclined to be acid.

Kelp burning used to be a flourishing industry in coastal regions where the large kelps flourished, but it is so no longer. At one time it was said that the Scilly Islanders had three industries: smuggling, wrecking, and kelp burning.

Kelp burning was first carried out for the sake of the soda in the ash of the kelps. Species of *Laminaria* and *Fucus* were used, as well as *Ascophyllum nodosum*, the knotted wrack. After the weeds had dried they were burned in kilns, the dried wracks being continuously fed in until there was a layer of ash from fifteen to twenty-four inches thick. Kelp burning for soda flourished extensively during the American War of Independence, and also during the Peninsular War, but a few years later two events happened which combined to kill the industry. The duty on imported barilla was reduced, and the salt tax was abolished altogether. Salt was a secondary product in burning kelp for soda. As a result of these two events kelp burning was no longer profitable, and the industry nearly came to an end.

The moribund kelp-burning trade received a new impetus when the French kelp burners, who used kelp ash as a source of potash, discovered that the ash also contained a great deal of iodine. This discovery gave new hope to the British trade, and not only were the existing kelp factories reorganized, but new ones were set up, especially on the coast of Scotland. For a time all was well. *Laminaria* was preferred to the wracks for burning, since its iodine content was higher, and the rate of burning was carefully controlled to prevent the volatilization of the iodine.

However, the kelp-burning industry was doomed. Beds of saltpetre were discovered in Chili from which iodine could be obtained much more cheaply than from seaweeds. This was the end of kelp burning in this country, though iodine is still obtained from seaweeds in Japan, where from five to seven per cent of the world's supply is produced.

Kelp burning was started up again on the Pacific coast of South America and Canada in 1910 as a means of obtaining potash, which was scarce at the time because of the difficulty of obtaining it from Germany. The giant kelps *Macrocystis*, *Nereocystis*, and *Alaria* were used. The seaweeds were harvested by special machinery, which cut the kelps under water and transferred them by conveyor belts to barges. The American kelp industry was profitable for a time, but after the First World War, when the German potash deposits at Stassfürt became available to America, there was no further need for kelp burning.

The story should end there, but it does not, though the present-day kelp industry is on entirely different lines from the old. As far back as 1883 an organic chemist called Stanford discovered that some of the brown seaweeds produced a sticky substance which gave a new compound when treated with carbonic acid. This compound was given the name alginic acid, and for the next fifty years it remained buried in the archives of organic chemistry.

In 1934 alginic acid suddenly achieved prominence, for it was found that it could be used in preparing transparent wrapping paper. A company was formed for the extraction of alginic acid from seaweed. Since then, many other uses for it have been found. It can be used for making artificial silk, as a stabilizer for ice-cream, for making plastic with which to take dental impressions; and as an improver for the soil it is superior to krillium. Gauze containing calcium alginate is used as a surgical dressing to prevent bleeding; alginates are also used in the food industry for the preparation of soups and sauces. Many other uses are likely to be found for this industrial Jack-of-all-trades, and the kelp trade is now on a more secure footing than ever before, and likely to remain so for a long time.

The use of certain red seaweeds for the preparation of agar-agar has already been mentioned. The traditional source of agar up to 1939 was the Japanese seaweed *Gelidium amansii*. With the outbreak of the Second World War supplies were cut off, and countries in the West had to look elsewhere. In Great Britain *Gigartina stellata* and *Chondrus crispus* were found to be satisfactory as agar producers, while in America *Gelidium cartilaginum*, *Gracilaria confervoides*, and *Hypnea confervoides* were preferred.

Besides its important function in preparing media for the cultivation of micro-organisms, agar has other minor uses. It is used in the canning of fish, in the manufacture of paper and glue, in the sizing of fabrics, in finishing of leather goods, in cooking as a thickening agent for ice-creams, and in brewing and wine-making as a clearing agent. It is also used in medicine as a laxative.

Even fossil seaweeds have their uses. Mention has been made of the large deposits of diatomaceous earth, or kieselgühr, found in several parts of the world, and consisting of the fossilized shells of diatoms. Some of these are of fresh-water origin, but others are marine; the latter include the great deposit at Lompoc, California, where the beds are over 700-feet thick and extend for miles.

Diatomaceous earth is used for a variety of purposes, and new uses are continually being found. Its traditional use is as a fine abrasive in toothpastes and silver polishes, and it was formerly used extensively as an absorbent for liquid nitro-glycerine in making dynamite. Today it is mainly used for filtering liquids, especially in the refining of sugar, and in the insulation of blast-furnaces and other structures when intense heat is generated. As an insulator it is greatly superior to asbestos, since it keeps its insulating power even at high temperatures, which asbestos does not. Another minor use is as an additive to paints used for painting traffic lanes on roads; it is said to improve their visibility at night.

```
*****
* 11 *
*****
```

Collecting and naming seaweeds

During Victorian times collecting seaweeds was a fashionable hobby, but today this pleasant habit seems to have lapsed. This is a pity, for the collection of seaweeds is one of the most satisfying ways of amusing oneself during a summer holiday by the sea, with the added zest that one may always come across a specimen that has not been recorded before in the locality. The chances of doing this with a flowering plant are slim, for too many people have always been there before, but the seaweeds have not been browsed over to anything like the same extent, and there is a real chance for an amateur, and even a beginner at that, to add to the store of scientific knowledge.

EQUIPMENT NEEDED
For the beginner, all that is really needed is a bucket of the kind used by children for making sand castles, plus an observant eye. Many an eminent algologist has started with nothing more than these. If, however, the seaweed collection is to mean more than a pleasant whiling away of a few idle hours on a seaside holiday, something more will be needed; not a great deal more, but just enough to equip one for serious phycology, as the study of seaweeds (and fresh-water algae) is called.

First, one should be properly clothed. Most of one's collecting is likely to be done while scrambling over rocks, especially near the low-tide mark, and rocks can be extremely slippery, particularly when covered with a wet growth of seaweed. Shorts or bathing trunks and canvas shoes with rope soles are the best things to wear for summer collecting; if one accidentally gets

167

a wetting it will be of no consequence. If one's interest extends to winter collecting, more extensive clothing will be needed, and a pair of thigh boots or, better still, fishermen's waders, will be a necessity.

If one is going to collect seaweeds from below the low-tide mark a boat and some form of dredge will be needed, unless one is an amateur skin-diver, in which case an aqualung is infinitely preferable.

The most convenient receptacle for specimens is a large plastic bag. Smaller bags should be included for some of the more delicate specimens, and also plastic tubes for really tiny seaweeds. Glass tubes should *never* be carried; they not only break easily, but broken glass can turn a minor fall into a nasty accident. The small tubes used nowadays by most chemists for housing pills are suitable.

Notes should be made at the time of collection of the location where specimens are found, so a small pad or notebook and a pencil should be carried. Do not use a pen, for ink runs when wet and can soon become indecipherable. A blunt knife for prising holdfasts free from rocks is essential, and if the collection is going to include calcareous seaweeds a geological hammer, or at least a hammer with a wedge-shaped (not pronged) reverse to its head will be needed.

A good hand lens, magnifying about ten times, is a useful piece of equipment. This should preferably have a single lens which can be swung inside a protecting cover when not in use. If you really want to be kind to yourself, get one of the more expensive aplanatic lenses; they are worth the extra money. Tie a cord round the hinge of the lens and wear it round your neck when collecting; it will then always be ready for use, and there will be no danger of dropping it down an inaccessible crack in the rocks.

If you are a photographer you will find photographing seaweeds where they grow quite fascinating. A 35-mm. single-lens reflex camera is ideal for the job. A short extension tube should be carried for close-ups, of which there will be many, and the lens should be fitted with a polarizing filter to cut out reflections when photographing submerged specimens.

COLLECTING SEAWEEDS

Little need be said about the actual process of collecting seaweeds. Having made a brief preliminary survey of the area to be
collected from, it is best to select a small part of it and go over
it really thoroughly. Most beginners try to survey far too wide
an area, with the result that the smaller and rarer plants tend
to be missed. "He that seeketh, findeth" should be the motto
of every collector. The rarer the seaweed the harder it is to spot,
so choose a small section of territory and look at every bit of
seaweed it contains. The thrill of finding a specimen of a seaweed
that is marked in the textbooks as "rare", or better still "very
rare", has to be experienced to be believed.

Always collect your plants whole and undamaged, even if
this means chipping away the rock with a hammer to free the
holdfast. Collect only perfect specimens. Where the form of the
frond changes with age it will be worthwhile collecting several
specimens of different ages.

Don't forget that some of the smaller seaweeds may grow
under larger ones. The shore may appear to be covered with
nothing but a solid mass of bladder wrack, but you may be
surprised at what you find when you lift the fronds of bladder
wrack and examine the rock beneath. Remember that many
species are epiphytes, growing on the stipes and the fronds of
other seaweeds. This is especially true in the lower littoral and
sublittoral zones.

PRESERVING AND MOUNTING THE SPECIMENS

It is possible to preserve seaweeds for the collection in three ways.

1. They may be pickled in a preserving fluid and kept in jars. For
microscopic and delicate filamentous forms this is the only possible
method. As a preservative, sea water containing five per cent of
formalin (obtainable quite cheaply at any chemist's shop) is
suitable. If sea water is not available, a substitute can be made
up by dissolving 3 oz. of Tidman's Sea Salt (chemist's shop
again) in half a gallon of water. Seaweeds preserved in this way
can be kept indefinitely in sealed jars.

2. The seaweed can be allowed to dry naturally in the air.
This will cause it to shrivel badly, but most seaweeds will regain
much of their original appearance if they are subsequently

6*

soaked in sea water or a solution of Tidman's Sea Salt before mounting permanently on herbarium sheets. This method should only be used in desperation.

3. The best method of preserving most seaweeds is to dry them in a press. This will prevent shrinking. The seaweed is washed in sea water or Tidman's solution to remove sand and debris and placed in sea water in a shallow white dish (the dishes used for developing photographic enlargements are ideal). The dish should be large enough to accommodate a sheet of mounting paper spread out flat.

The mounting paper should be smooth, unglazed, and thick. Herbarium sheets of standard size (16 x 11 in.) can be bought from any supplier of biological materials, such as Flatter & Garnet of Manchester, or Gerrard of London, or the collector can make his own from good-quality cartridge paper, which will serve equally well. Any size of sheet can be used, but the sheets should not be too small, or difficulty will be experienced in arranging large specimens.

A piece of mounting paper is submerged in sea water in the dish, and the washed specimen placed on top of it. The parts of the specimen are spread out by means of a small brush or needle so as to display them to their best advantage. Bushy specimens may want a little trimming here and there, using a sharp pair of scissors.

The paper carrying the specimen is then carefully lifted from the water, taking care that the seaweed does not become disarranged in the process. This is the only part of the process where skill is needed, which can only be gained by experience. The paper is best lifted in a slightly sloping position, with the base of the specimen upwards, so that the water drains off it into the dish. If the specimen should slip during the lifting it is best to reimmerse the paper and start again. As with everything else, practice will make perfect, and the beginner must expect some failures at first.

The mounted specimen is laid on a sheet of drying paper, covered with muslin, and another sheet of drying paper placed on top of it. Drying paper can be obtained from a firm of biological suppliers, or blotting paper can be used; even two or three sheets of newspaper will do at a pinch. The whole process is then repeated with more specimens, piling one on top of another, separated by sheets of drying paper. If the pile is very large a sheet of corrugated cardboard here and there between the drying sheets will help aeration and therefore drying.

Finally, the pile of specimens and drying paper should be placed between boards under a weight. The weight should not be too heavy, or damage may result; the heavy weights used in drying flowering plants are too much for seaweeds. The exact weight can only be found by experience, but three or four moderately heavy books should be sufficient. Alternatively, pressure can be applied by placing a pair of straps round the boards; these have the advantage that, if the pressing is done during a holiday, the press with its pile of specimens can by put into the boot of a car when it is time to go home without fear of disturbing the collections.

The drying papers will need to be changed after about twelve hours, and then daily until the specimens are dry which, at normal British temperatures, will be in about a week. They can then be taken out of the press. Many of the seaweeds will have stuck to the paper by virtue of their own mucilage, and so will need no further treatment. Those that have not stuck should be fixed in place with narrow bands of sticky paper.

The last thing to do is to label the specimens. Special herbarium labels can be obtained at little cost from a biological supplier, or the information can be written straight on to the bottom right-hand corner of the herbarium sheet. The label should include the name of the seaweed, its family, the locality where it was collected, and the date. Any other useful information may be included, such as the name of the collector, the authority on which the identification was founded, the position on the shore (e.g. high, mid, or low littoral), the substratum on which it was growing (sand, rock, epiphyte, etc.). With an epiphyte, the name of the host should be included.

GIVING IT A NAME
Naming seaweeds correctly is a difficult business; I wish I could say it were not, but that would be a lie that would make Ananias blush. Only the toadstools are more difficult to name than the seaweeds—by a very small margin!

I say this, not to put you off (Heaven forbid) but merely to warn you that you will not find the naming of your specimens easy, and that you are bound to fail altogether with some of them. If you do, you will fail in good company, for every professional botanist has to go to an expert on the particular group for some of his identifications, and sometimes even the expert is foxed.

If you cannot arrive at the correct species, you will probably be able to arrive at the genus. This will do for your herbarium label for the time being; later on you may, as you grow more expert, be able to add the species. The great thing is never to guess; if you are not sure, leave the label blank until you are sure. You will be surprised how, with practice, your power of naming seaweeds will improve. We all had to start from scratch some time.

I am going to name three books which will help. The standard work on the identification of seaweeds from this country is *A Handbook of the British Seaweeds*, by Lily Newton (British Museum, 1931). This excellent book is comprehensive and contains many fine illustrations (a great help). For the beginner it has three snags: it is written for the expert, in technical language; a microscope is needed to follow out some of the identifications; and many of the names have changed over the last forty years.

The next book is *British Seaweeds*, by Carola Dickinson (Eyre and Spottiswoode, 1963). This deals only with the larger seaweeds (by "larger" I mean those that can be seen with the naked eye).It is excellently written in popular language that the beginner can cope with, the illustrations are first class, and it contains a wealth of information about the history of seaweeds, making it eminently readable. It is by no means comprehensive, but it contains descriptions of all the species that a beginner is likely to find. If you are going to get one book only on the identification of seaweeds, this is the one.

Finally, there is *Collins Pocket Guide to the Sea Shore*, by Barrett and Yonge (Collins, 1958). This excellent book provides a bonus in that it describes all the life of the sea shore, animal as well as plant. The seaweeds form only a short section of the book, which is mainly devoted to animals, but the section on seaweeds is well done, and there are plenty of illustrations, both coloured and black and white.

One (or, better still, all) of these books will set your feet on the right pathway and should solve your immediate difficulties. If you get really stuck, the Marine Biology Laboratory at Plymouth, or the seaweed section at the British Museum of Natural History are the places where you are most likely to get help.

APPENDIX

Cells and cell division

Seaweeds, like most plants, are built up from tiny units called cells, as a house is built of bricks. A cell consists of a jelly-like material called protoplasm, which is the essential living matter of the cell. Within the general protoplasm of the cell is a dense, spherical or ovoid body called the nucleus, which is regarded as being a part of the protoplasm. The term cytoplasm is used for that part of the protoplasm which is not included in the nucleus.

Most plant cells are bounded by a more-or-less rigid cell wall, usually constructed of a carbohydrate called cellulose. The cytoplasm generally forms a lining just inside the cell wall. Most of the internal part of the cell is taken up by a space, the vacuole, filled with fluid called the cell sap.

The nucleus is a most important part of the cell. Not only does it appear to direct the cell in performing some of its vital functions, but it also is the carrier of hereditary information. This information is carried on the molecules of deoxyribonucleic acid, or D.N.A., which make up an important part of the rod-like bodies, or chromosomes, which are found in the nucleus.

For every species of animal or plant the number of chromosomes in every nucleus is the same. The chromosomes are paired: there are two of each kind of chromosome in every cell. This is known as the diploid number, and the cell or nucleus bearing the diploid number of chromosomes is said to be diploid. When a cell divides into two the nucleus also divides, and when it does so each chromosome is cut lengthways into two exactly similar halves, one half going to each of the daughter nuclei. In this way the chromosome number characteristic of the species is maintained, and the daughter nuclei formed by the division of a nucleus get identical sets of chromosomes. This method of division is called mitosis.

175

When two nuclei fuse in sexual reproduction the chromosomes do not fuse. In order to prevent doubling of the chromosome number each time sexual reproduction occurs, the number is halved some time before the sexual act. A cell division occurs in which the chromosomes do not split; instead, one member of each similar pair goes to each daughter nucleus. This kind of division is called meiosis, and a cell or nucleus containing half the normal number of chromosomes (i.e. one chromosome from each similar pair) is said to be haploid.

In animals, and in some plants, meiosis usually immediately precedes the formation of the sex cells or gametes. In most plants meiosis occurs earlier than this.

GLOSSARY

Terms of little importance that have been mentioned only once in the text have, in general, been omitted from the Glossary.

Akinete. A form of non-motile spore found in some of the blue-green algae.

Alternation of generations. The regular alternation of a sporophyte, or spore-bearing generation, with a gametophyte, or sexual generation.

Antheridium. An organ in which male gametes are formed.

Auxiliary cell. A cell, not the carpogonium, from which, in some red seaweeds, the gonimoblast filaments arise.

Auxospore. A special kind of spore formed by the diatoms, in some cases as a result of sexual reproduction. The formation of auxospores restores the normal size of the organism.

Benthos. The life of the sea bottom.

Carotene. One of the series of pigments contained in the chloroplasts of plants.

Carpogonium. The female sex organ in the red seaweeds.

Carpospore. A spore formed as a result of the fertilization of the egg-cell in the carpogonium of a red seaweed.

Carposporophyte. The generation that bears the carpospores in the red seaweeds.

Chlorophyll. The green pigment in the chloroplasts of plants that makes photosynthesis possible.

Chloroplast. A solid cell-inclusion containing chlorophyll.

Chromatic adaptation. The assistance of photosynthesis by the use of pigments that absorb the energy of light but are not themselves photosynthetic.

Chromatophore. A solid cell-inclusion containing pigment.

Chromosome. One of the bodies in the nuclei of cells on which hereditary information is carried.

Coenocyte. A multinucleate structure in which the individual nuclei are not separated by cell walls.

Conceptacle. A usually flask-shaped cavity in which the sex organs are housed in some of the seaweeds, especially the Fucales.

Cortex. The outer layers of the stipe or frond of a seaweed.

Diploid. Having the double chromosome number.

Epiphyte. A plant that grows on another plant.

Epitheca. The top half of the frustule of a diatom.

Flagellum. One of the whip-like protoplasmic extensions by which some cells are able to swim.

Frustule. The highly silicified shell of a diatom.

Fucoxanthin. A brown pigment, found especially in the chromatophores of the brown seaweeds and the diatoms.

Gamete. One of the two cells that fuse in sexual reproduction.

Gametophyte. The sexual generation in most plants.

Gas vacuole. A type of vacuole found in many Cyanophyta and believed to contain gas.

Girdle. The sides of the frustule in a diatom. Also, the groove in the shell of a dinoflagellate in which the transverse flagellum is placed.

Gonimoblast filament. One of the filaments that, in most of the red seaweeds, bear the carposporangia.

Haploid. Having the single chromosome number.

Heterocyst. A large cell that, in blue-green algae, is often associated with the breaking of the filament into hormogonia.

Heteromorphic. Appertaining to an alternation of generations where the sporophyte differs structurally from the gametophyte.

Heterotrichus filament. A filament in which a prostrate part is differentiated from an upright part or parts.

Holdfast. The lower part of the stipe in a seaweed that is differentiated to act as a point of securement to the substratum.

Hormogonia. The portions into which a filamentous blue-green alga breaks up on reproduction.

Hypotheca. The lower part of the frustule of a diatom.

Isomorphic. Appertaining to an alternation of generations where the sporophyte resembles the gametophyte structurally.

Kelp. A term often loosely used to describe any large brown seaweed, but which should properly be kept for a member of the Laminariales.

Littoral zone. The region on the foreshore that lies between high and low-tide marks. Also sometimes used for the whole of the zone where land and sea meet.

Medulla. The central zone in the stipe or frond of a seaweed.

Meiosis. The type of nuclear division as a result of which the chromosome number is halved.

Metachromatic granules. The granules in the cells of blue-green algae that are believed to carry out some of the functions of a nucleus.

Microspores. Minute spores produced by some centric diatoms.

Mitosis. The type of nuclear division by which the chromosomes are distributed equally between the two daughter nuclei without reduction in chromosome number.

Monosiphoneous filament. The type of filament occurring in the red seaweeds where the central strand is not surrounded by pericentral cells.

Multiaxial filament. The type of frond, found in some of the red seaweeds, where there are several parallel filaments running longitudinally.

Nannoplankton. The term used to describe extremely small planktonic organisms.

Nurse cell. The cell into which the fertilized nucleus of the carpogonium passes in some of the red seaweeds.

Oöblast. A tubular outgrowth from the base of the carpogonium in certain red seaweeds through which the fertilized nucleus, or its derivatives, pass into the auxiliary cell.

Oögonium. The female sex organ in seaweeds.

Paraphysis. One of the hairs that may be formed between the reproductive organs in seaweeds.

Pericentral cell. One of the cells surrounding the main filament in polysiphoneous red seaweeds.

Photosynthesis. The process by which green plants make sugar from carbon dioxide and water, by the aid of chlorophyll and sunlight.

Phycocyanin. A blue pigment contained in the chromatophores of red seaweeds, and in the chromoplasm of blue-green algae.

Phycoerythrin. A red pigment contained in the chromatophores of red seaweeds.

Phytoplankton. That section of the plankton which consists of plants.

Plankton. The organisms, animal and plant, that float freely in the water, carried about by water currents.

Plurilocular sporangium. A sporangium which is divided into two or more cells.

Polysiphoneous filament. A filament in which the main central filament is surrounded by pericentral cells; found in some of the red seaweeds.

Raphe. A groove, containing cytoplasm, running longitudinally down the centre of one or both frustules in a pennate diatom.

Receptacle. The structure in which the conceptacles are housed, especially in the Fucales.

Spermatium. A male gamete of the red algae.

Spermogonium. A cell in which a spermatium is formed.

Sporangium. A structure in which spores are formed.

Spore. A non-sexual reproductive cell of a seaweed.

Sporocarp. The structure that surrounds the carpospores in some of the red seaweeds. Also, the fruit body containing the carpospores.

Stipe. The stalk supporting the frond of a seaweed.

Sulcus. The groove containing the longitudinal flagellum in a dinoflagellate.

Supporting cell. The cell that bears the carpogonium in a red seaweed.

Tetrasporangium. A sporangium containing tetraspores.

Tetraspore. A spore, one of a group of four, formed usually, though not always, following meiosis.

Trichogyne. The elongated terminal portion of the carpogonium in a red seaweed.

Trichome. A single row of cells in the filament of a blue-green alga.

Trumpet hyphae. Filaments in the stipe or frond of one of the Laminariales, having wide ends.

Uniaxial filament. The type of construction in the frond of a red seaweed where there is only one main filament and growing point.

Unilocular sporangium. A sporangium which is not divided by septa into several cells.

Vacuole. A space within a cell containing cell sap.

Valve. The top or bottom of the frustule in a diatom.

Wrack. A term loosely employed for any of the larger brown seaweeds, but which should strictly be confined to a member of the Fucales.

Xanthophyll. An orange-yellow pigment contained in the chloroplasts of plants.

Zonation. The arrangement of seaweeds in a number of different zones on the shore.

Zoöspore. A motile spore.

Zygote. The cell formed by the fusion of two gametes.

SELECTED BOOK-LIST

Barrett, J. H. and Yonge, C. M. *Collins Pocket Guide to the Sea Shore* (Collins, 1958).

Chapman, V. J. *The Algae* (Macmillan, 1962).

Dickinson, C. I. *British Seaweeds* (Eyre and Spottiswoode, 1963).

Duddington, C. L. *Beginner's Guide to Botany* (Pelham Books, 1970).

Duddington, C. L. *Seaweeds and Other Algae* (Faber and Faber, 1966).

Fritsch, F. E. *The Structure and Reproduction of the Algae* (Cambridge University Press, 1935).

Hardy, Sir Alister. *The Open Sea* (Collins, 1958).

Newton, L. *A Handbook of the British Seaweeds* (British Museum (Natural History), 1931).

Round, F. E. *The Biology of the Algae* (Arnold, 1965).

Yonge, C. M. *The Sea Shore* (Collins, 1949).

Index

185